Practical Guide to Versification

With a Compendious Dictionary, Examination of Classical Measures, and Comments Upon Burlesque and

Comic Verse, Vers de Société, and Song-writing

Tom Hood

Alpha Editions

This edition published in 2024

ISBN 9789361476440

Design and Setting By

Alpha Editions

www.alphaedis.com

Email - info@alphaedis.com

Contents

PREFACE.

I am anxious at the first outset that the object of this work should not be misunderstood. It does not assume to be a handbook for poets, or a guide to poetry. The attempt to compile such a book as is implied by either of those titles would be as absurd as pretentious.

A Poet, to paraphrase the Latin, is created, not manufactured. Cicero's "nascimur poetæ, fimus oratores," is, with some modification, even more to the point. In a word, poetical genius is a gift, but education and perseverance will make almost any man a versifier.

All, therefore, that this book aims to teach is the art of Versification. That art, like Logic, is "ars instrumentalis, dirigens mentem inter cognitionem rerum." As Logic does not supply you with arguments, but only defines the mode in which they are to be expressed or used, so Versification does not teach you how to write poetry, but how to construct verse. It may be a means to the end, but it does not pretend to assure its attainment. Versification and Logic are to Poetry and Reason what a parapet is to a bridge: they do not convey you across, but prevent you from falling over. The difference is that which exists between τεχνη and ἐπιστήμη.

This definition is rendered necessary by the Dogberry spirit which is now abroad, and which insists that "to be a well-favoured man is the gift of fortune,"—fortune in the sense of wealth, I presume,—"but to write and read comes by nature;" in fact, that to be "a poet" a man needs to be advantageously placed in the world, but that any one can "write poetry."

With this conviction, I have discarded the title of a guide for "Poets," feeling that there is much real poetry that is not in verse, and a vast deal of verse that is not poetry; and that therefore "a hard and fast line" was of the first importance to mark the boundary of my undertaking. Poetry is far less a question of manner than of matter, whereas versification is purely a question of form. I will even venture to say that some of our noblest poems are in prose; and that many great poets have been but inferior versifiers. But what these last wrote has possessed qualities compared with which the mere mechanism of their verse is as nothing. The poet gives to the world in his sublime thoughts diamonds of the purest water. It would be idle to quibble about minor points of the polishing and setting of such gems— they would lose in the process! But the writer of verse does not—and should not—pretend to give us diamonds. He offers paste-brilliants; and therefore it the more behoves him to see to the perfection of the cutting, on which their beauty depends.

The thoughts presented by the poet may be rough-hewn; the fancies of the versifier must be accurately finished, and becomingly set. Poetry, therefore, abounds in licences, while Versification boasts only of laws.

To enumerate, explain, and define these laws is the object of this work. Nor is such a task a waste of time, as those may be inclined to think, who argue that if one cannot write poetry, 'tis absurd to try to write verse. Yet versification is an elegant accomplishment to say the least—"emollit mores, nec sinit esse feros." But it is something more than an elegant accomplishment—much more.

In the dead languages—leaving in abeyance the question of classical *versus* mathematical education—nothing gives such scholarly finish as the practice of Greek and Latin verse-writing, nothing such an intimate knowledge and understanding of the genius of either language.

Were English versification taught in our schools, I believe the boys would acquire a better understanding and appreciation of their own tongue. With such training, a lad would shrink from a mispronunciation as he does from a false quantity in Latin or Greek. He would not fall into the slipshod way of pronouncing "doing" as if it were spelt "doin'," "again" as if "agen," and "written and spoken" as if "writtun and spokun." He would not make dissyllables of words like "fire" and "mire," or of the trisyllable "really." Nor would he make another mistake (very common now, as revealed in magazine verse where such words are put to rhyme, "before" and "more") of pronouncing "ure" as "ore,"—"shore" and "asshore" for "sure" and "assure," of which, of course, the correct pronunciation is "shewre," "ashewre."[1]

The purging of our pronunciation would be of general benefit. At present it is shifting and uncertain—because it is never taught. The dropping of the "h" is almost the only error in pronunciation that is ever noticed at school; and there being no standard set up, the pronunciation of English becomes every day more and more degraded by the mere force of the majority of uneducated vulgar. The Americanising of our language—which seems to me a less remote and no less undesirable possibility than "the Americanising of our institutions," about which we hear so much—can only be checked by some such educational system. Surely the deterioration of our language is not a minor matter, and when it can be removed by the encouragement of verse-writing at our schools, strictly and clearly taught, it seems astonishing that no effort has been made in that direction.[2]

However, whether, by establishing a system of English versifying at our schools, we shall ever endeavour to give fixity to our pronunciation, is a question hardly likely, I fear, to be brought to the test yet awhile. That English versifying is a strong educational power, I do not doubt, and in that belief, have endeavoured to render this handbook as complete as possible. I have therefore laid down the most stringent rules and the clearest formulæ in my power.

Verse is but the A B C of Poetry, and the student must learn his alphabet correctly. We should not allow a child to arrange the letters as he chose,— "A, Z, B, G, C,"—nor must the beginner in verse dream of using any licences of a similar kind. I should fail in my duty if I admitted anything of the kind; for while it would be presumption to lay down laws for poets, it would be incapacity to frame licences for versifiers.

I therefore conclude these prefatory remarks by adducing the two chief regulations for the student.

First, That he must use such rhymes only as

are perfect to the ear, when correctly pronounced.

Second, That he must never write a line

which will not sooner or later in the

stanza have a line to correspond with a rhyme.

To these I may add, as a rider, this piece of advice (somewhat in the style of the whist maxim, "When in doubt, play a trump"): If you have reason to choose between two styles of versification, select the more difficult.

It is only by sustaining your verse at the highest elevation that you can hope even to approach poetry.

"Be bold—be bold—but not too bold!"

And bear in mind the words of Sir Philip Sidney:—"Who shootes at the midday Sonne, though he be sure he shall neuer hit the marke; yet as sure he is, he shall shoote higher than who aymes but at a bush."

T. H.

CHAPTER I.

VERSE GENERALLY.

There is no better text for this chapter than some lines from Pope's "Essay on Criticism":—

"But most by numbers judge a poet's song,

And smooth or rough, with them, is right or wrong:

These equal syllables alone require,

Tho' oft the ear the open vowels tire;

While expletives their feeble aid do join;

And ten low words oft creep in one dull line:

While they ring round the same unvaried chimes,

With sure returns of still recurring rhymes;

Where'er you find 'the cooling western breeze,'

In the next line it 'whispers through the trees:'

If crystal streams 'with pleasing murmurs creep,'

The reader's threaten'd—not in vain—with 'sleep.'

Then at the last and only couplet, fraught

With some unmeaning thing they call a thought,

A needless Alexandrine ends the song,

That like a wounded snake, drags its slow length along.

Leave such to tune their own dull rhymes, to know

What's roundly smooth, or languishingly slow;

And praise the easy vigour of a line

Where Denham's strength, and Waller's sweetness join.

True ease in writing comes from art, not chance,

As those move easiest who have learnt to dance.

'Tis not enough no harshness gives offence,

The sound must seem an echo to the sense.

Soft is the strain when zephyr gently blows,

And the smooth stream in smoother numbers flows;

But when loud surges lash the sounding shore,

The hoarse rough verse should like the torrent roar:

When Ajax strives some rock's vast weight to throw,

The line, too, labours, and the words move slow.

Not so, when swift Camilla scours the plain,

Flies o'er th' unbending corn, and skims along the main."

Johnson sneers somewhat at the attempt at what he styles "representative metre." He quotes "one of the most successful attempts,"—

"With many a weary step, and many a groan,

Up a high hill he heaves a huge round stone;

The huge round stone, resulting with a bound,

Thunders impetuous down and smokes along the ground."

After admitting that he sees the stone move slowly upward, and roll violently back, he says, "try the same numbers to another sense—

"While many a merry tale and many a song

Cheer'd the rough road, we wish'd the rough road long.

The rough road then returning in a round

Mock'd our impatient steps, for all was fairy ground."

"We have now," says the Doctor, "lost much of the delay and much of the rapidity." Truly so!—but why? The choice of words has really altered the measure, though not the number of syllables. If we look at the second line of the first extract, we see how the frequent use of the aspirate, with a long sound after it, gives the labour of the ascent. There is nothing of this in the corresponding line, where the "r" gives a run rather than a halt to the measure. But Johnson more decidedly shows how he was mistaken when he finds fault with Pope's—

"The varying verse, the full resounding line,

The long majestic march, and energy divine."

His objection to this is, that the same sequence of syllables gives "the rapid race" and "the march of slow-paced majesty;" and he adds, "the exact prosodist will find the line of *swiftness* by one time longer than that of *tardiness*." By this it is to be presumed he alludes to the trisyllabic nature of the first foot of the first line—"varying." But it is just that which gives the rapidity. The other half of the line is not meant to give rapidity, but "resounding." The second line, by the repetition of the "a" in "march" and "majesty," gives the tramp of the march to admiration.

So much for Johnson's objections. We will now see how far the lines of Pope can guide us in the construction of verse.

LINE THIRD indicates the necessity—which Pope himself, even, did not adequately recognise—the necessity of varying the fall of the verse on the ear. Pope did this by graduating his accents. The line should scan with an accented syllable following an unaccented one—

"And smo´oth or ro´ugh, with the´m, is ri´ght or wro´ng."

Pope varied this by a sort of compromise—

"And the´ smooth strea´m in smo´other nu´mbers flo´ws,"

would be the right scansion. But the accent passes in a subdued form from "the" to "smooth," which pleasantly modulates the line, and gives the flow required for the figure treated of.[3]

But there was another means of varying the verse which was not in those days adopted. It was not then recognised that there were some cases in which the unaccented syllable might have two "beats." Pope wrote,

"The gen'rous pleasure to be charm'd with wit."

Had he written "generous," it might have stood, and would have given a variety. And this would have saved the eyesore of such lines as—

"T' admire superior sense and doubt our own."

LINE FOURTH does not exactly describe the fault it commits. "The open vowel" is no offence, but rather a beauty, though like all beauty it must not be too lavishly displayed. The fault of the line really lies in the repetition of the same broad sound—"o." The same vowel-sounds should not be repeated in a line.[4] This especially holds good where they are so associated with consonants as to form a rhyme, or anything approaching to it.

LINE FIFTH points out an inelegance which no one with any ear could be guilty of—the use of "do" and "did," to eke out a line or help a rhyme.

LINE SIXTH indicates a practice which those who have studied Latin versification would avoid without such a hint, since the nature of the cæsura compels the avoidance of monosyllables.

LINE NINTH, with the following three lines, warns against an error which naturally becomes the more frequent the longer English verse is written, since rhymes become more and more hackneyed every day.

LINE SIXTEENTH. The Alexandrine will come under discussion in its place among metres.

LINE TWENTY-FIRST might well serve for a motto for this little treatise. If a poet said this of poetry, how much more does it apply to versification!

LINE TWENTY-FIFTH. Here, and in the following line, by delicate manipulation of the accent, Pope gets the desired effect. Instead of "So so´ft the stra´in," he attracts the ear with "So´ft is," and the unexpected word gives the key-note of the line.

LINE TWENTY-SEVENTH. It is almost needless to point out how in this, and the next line, the poet, by artful management of accent and careful selection of onomatopoetic words, gives the required assonance to the lines.

LINE TWENTY-NINTH. The broad vowels here give the requisite pause and "deliberation" to the verse. In the following line, the introduction of "too"—(under some circumstances it might well come under the condemnation of Line Fifth)—makes the line labour, and the open "o" at the end of the line "tires the ear."

LINE THIRTY-FIRST. Here the poet gets the slide of the "s" to give the idea of motion. In the following line by the elision and the apt introduction of short syllables he repeats the notion. In my opinion the artistic skill of Pope is peculiarly observable in the last few couplets. In the first line in each instance the effect is produced by the use of a different artifice from that employed in the second.

These rules were of course intended by Pope to apply only to the measure called "heroic," *i.e.*, decasyllabic verse. But, *mutatis mutandis*, they will be equally applicable to general verse.

Coleridge in his "Christabel" struck out what he considered a new metre, which he describes as "not, properly speaking, irregular, though it may seem so from its being founded on a new principle: namely, that of counting in each line the accents, not the syllables. Though the latter may vary from seven to twelve, yet in each line the accents will be found to be only four." This was a decided step in the right direction, being in truth a recognition of the principle that measure in English was not exhausted—

was, indeed, hardly satisfied—by the old rule of thumb; that, in short, it needed a compromise between *accent* and *quantity*.

Southey in his "Thalaba" essayed a new style of versification, of which he writes as follows:—

"It were easy to make a parade of learning by enumerating the various feet which it admits; it is only needful to observe that no two lines are employed in sequence, which can be read into one. Two six-syllable lines (it will perhaps be answered) compose an Alexandrine; the truth is, that the Alexandrine, when harmonious, is composed of two six-syllable lines. One advantage this metre assuredly possesses; the dullest reader cannot distort it into discord.... I do not wish the *improvisatore* time, but something that denotes the sense of harmony; something like the accent of feeling; like the tone which every poet necessarily gives to poetry."

Of course, by "six syllables" Southey means "six feet." He was evidently struggling for emancipation from the old rule of thumb.

Of late many eccentricities of versification have been attempted after the manner of Mr Whitman, but for these, like the Biblical echo of Mr Tupper's muse, there seem to be no perceptible rules, even should it be desirable to imitate them.

I would here add a few words of advice to those who, by the study of our greatest writers, would endeavour to improve their own style. For smoothness I should say Waller, in preference even to Pope, because the former wrote in far more various measures, and may challenge comparison with Pope, on Pope's own ground, with "The Ode to the Lord Protector," in decasyllabic verse. For music—"lilt" is an expressive word that exactly conveys what I mean—they cannot do better than choose Herrick. Add to these two George Herbert, and I think the student will have a valuable guide in small space.

CHAPTER II.

CLASSIC VERSIFICATION.

There is little doubt that the best and easiest way of learning English grammar is through the Latin. That English versification cannot be similarly acquired through the Latin is due to the fact that the Latin system depends on quantity, and the English chiefly on accent and rhyme. Nevertheless, a slight acquaintance with the classic measures will prove useful to the student of English verse. In the absence of all teaching of English versification at our schools, they have done good service in giving our boys some insight into the structure of verse.

The structure of Latin and Greek verse depends on the quantity—the length or shortness expressed by the forms — ⏑. A long syllable is equal in duration to two short syllables, which may therefore take its place (as it may take theirs) in certain positions. The combinations of syllables are called feet, of which there are about nine-and-twenty. Twelve of the most common are here given:—

Spondee	— —
Pyrrhic	⏑ ⏑
Trochee	— ⏑
Iambus	⏑ —
Molossus	— — —
Tribrach	⏑ ⏑ ⏑
Dactyl	— ⏑ ⏑
Anapæst	⏑ ⏑ —
Bacchic	⏑ — —
Antibacchic	— — ⏑
Amphimacer	— ⏑ —
Amphibrach	⏑ — ⏑

Of the styles of verse produced by combinations of these feet the most important are the Heroic, or Hexameter; the Elegiac, alternate Hexameters and Pentameters; and the Dramatic or Iambic. All others may be classed as Lyrics.

The Cæsura (division) is the separation of each verse into two parts by the ending of a word in the middle of a certain foot.[5] It may be here noted that this principle (the ending of a word in the middle of a foot) applies generally to the verse, it being an inelegance to construct lines of words of which each constitutes a foot. The well-known line of Virgil, marked to show the feet, will explain this at a glance—

"Arma vi | rumque ca | no | | Tro | jæ qui | primus ab | oris."

In this the cæsura occurs in the third foot, between *cano* and *Trojæ*. But in no case is one foot composed of one word only.

The Hexameter line consists of, practically, five dactyls and a spondee or trochee. A spondee may take the place of each of the first four dactyls— and sometimes, but very rarely, of the fifth. The cæsura falls in the third foot at the end of the first—and sometimes at the end of the second— syllable of the dactyl. In some cases it is in the fourth foot, after the first syllable. The last word in the line should be either a dissyllable or trisyllable.

The Pentameter is never used alone, but, with a Hexameter preceding it in the distich, forms Elegiac Verse. It consists of two parts, divided by a cæsura, each part composed of two dactyls (interchangeable with spondees) and a long syllable.[6] The last place in the line should be occupied by a dissyllabic word—at least it should not be a monosyllable or trisyllable.

The Iambic is most commonly used in a six-foot line of iambics (the trimeter iambic, *vide* note on last paragraph). In the first, third, and fifth place a spondee may be substituted, and there are other licenses which we need not here enter upon, as the measure is not of much importance for our purposes. The cæsura occurs in the third or fourth foot.

The Lyrics are, as a rule, compound verses; different sorts of feet enter into the formation of the lines; and the stanzas consist of lines of different kinds, and are styled strophes.

The chief of the lyric measures are the Sapphic and Alcaic.

The Sapphic is a combination of three Sapphic verses with an Adonic.

Lines 1, 2, 3, — ☐ | — — | — || ☐ ☐ | — ☐ | — ☐ | — —☐

Line 4, — ☐ ☐ | — —

The double line represents the cæsura, which in rare instances falls a syllable later.

The Alcaic is, like the Sapphic, a four-line stanza. Its scheme is—

Lines 1 and 2, —□ — | □ — | — || — □ □ | — □ —□

Line 3, —□ — | □ — | — — | □ — | —□

Line 4, — □ □ | — □ □ | — □ | — —□

That is to say, it consists of two eleven-syllable, one nine-syllable, and one ten-syllable Alcaic lines (Alcaici hendeka-, ennea-, and deka-syllabici). Much of the success of the stanza depends on the flow of the third line, which, according to the best models, should consist of three trisyllables (or equivalent combinations, *e.g.* a dissyllable noun with its monosyllabic preposition).

When it is stated that Horace wrote in four or five-and-twenty lyric measures, it will be obvious that I cannot exhaust, or attempt to exhaust, the list of measures in a work like this. The reader will have acquired some notion of the nature of classic versification, from what I have stated of Latin composition applying with unimportant differences to Greek. Those who have the leisure or the inclination might do worse than study Greek and Latin poetry, if only to see if they can suggest no novelties of metre. I can recall no English verse that reproduces Horace's musical measure:—

"Mĭsĕrār' est | nĕqu' ămōrī dărĕ lūdūm | nĕqŭe dūlcī

Mălă vīnō | lăvĕr' āut ēx|ănĭmārī | mĕtŭēntēs

Pătrŭǣ vēr| bĕră līnguǣ."

Greek verse seems a less promising field than Latin at a first glance. But one of the choruses in Aristophanes's "Plutus" has an exact echo in English verse.

"ἄνδρες φίλοι κἀι δημόται κἀι τοῦ πονεῖν ἐρασταί."

may fairly run in a curricle with

"A captain bold of Halifax who lived in country quarters."

The great difficulty of finding a corresponding measure in English for Latin or Greek verse, on the accepted theory that the English acute accent answers to the Latin long quantity, and the grave accent to the short, will be found in the spondee. We have no means of replacing the two longs in juxtaposition, and are compelled to find refuge in what, according to the accent-quantity theory, is either an iamb or a trochee.

I subjoin the following attempts to render a few Latin metres, commencing with a translation of the Horatian measure just alluded to:—

"Hapless lasses who in glasses may not drown those pangs of passion,

Or disclose its bitter woes, it's—so they tell you—not the fashion."

Yet this, in spite of the sub-rhymes which give the swing of the Ionicus (☐ ☐ — ´ —) may well be read as a succession of trochees—that is to say, according to the quantity-accent system.

Here is an attempt at the Sapphic:—

"Never—ah me—now, as in days aforetime

Rises o'erwhelming memory—'tis banish'd!

Scenes of loved childhood, cannot ye restore time,

Though it has vanish'd?"

The Alcaic measure is essayed in the following:—

"Ah woe! the men who gallantly sallying

Strode forth undaunted, rapidly rallying—

No longer advancing attack-ward,

Rush'd a disorderly tumult backward."

In these, again, the difficulty of exactly replacing quantity by accent is great—if not insurmountable. Hence it is that, as a rule, the attempts at giving the exact reproductions of Latin measures have failed. Nevertheless I believe that corresponding measures, suitable to the genius of our language, may be suggested by a study of the classics.

The often-quoted lines of Coleridge on the hexameter and pentameter appear to me faulty:—

"In the hex|ameter | rises || the | fountain's | silvery | column—

In the pen|tameter | aye || falling in | melody | back."

The first feet of both lines are less dactyls than anapæsts. The cæsura of the first line is not the "worthier" cæsura. In the second line the monosyllable is inadmissible in the last place.

Here I may as well point out what seems to me to be a difficulty of English versification which has given much trouble. The substitution of accent for quantity is not all that is required to make the best verse. Quantity enters into the consideration too. A combination of consonants, giving an almost imperceptible weight to the vowel preceding them, goes far to disqualify it for a place as an unaccented syllable. To my thinking "rises a" would be a better English dactyl than "rises the," and "falls it in" than "falling in." But no agglomeration of consonants can make such a syllable accented. Two lines from Coleridge's "Mahomet" will evidence this—

"Huge wasteful | empires | founded and | hallowed | slow

perse | cution,

Soul-wither | ing but | crush'd the | blasphemous | rites of

the | Pagan."

"Huge wasteful" is not a dactyl, and "ing but" is certainly not a spondee—nor is "crushed the." "Hallowed," by force of the broad "o," is almost perfect as a spondee, on the other hand; as is "empires" also. Longfellow, in his "Evangeline," has perhaps done the best that can be done to give an exact rendering of the Latin hexameter; but Tennyson, in portions of "Maud," has caught its spirit, and transfused it into an English form. No poet, indeed, has done so much as the Laureate to introduce new or revive old forms of versification, and enrich the language with musical measure.

It may be well to note here that the classic poets did not forget the use of the maxim which Pope expresses in the line—

"The sound must seem an echo to the sense."

In this they were greatly assisted by the use of the quantity, which enabled them the more readily to give rapidity or weight to their lines. Nothing could more admirably represent a horse's gallop than the beat of the words—

"Quadrupedante putrem sonittu quatit ungula campum."

The unwieldiness of the Cyclops is splendidly shadowed in the line—

"Monstrum, horrendum, informe, ingens cui lumen ademptum."

And again the beat of the Cyclopean hammers is well imitated in the verse—

"Illi inter sese magnâ vi brachia tollunt."

Too much stress may easily be laid on this adornment, and some poets have carried it to excess. But the beginner in verse will do well not to overlook it.

NOTE.—The Poet Laureate, whose mastery of metre is remarkable, has given us alcaics in his lines to Milton—

"Oh, mighty-mouth'd inventor of harmonies,

Oh, skill'd to sing of time and eternity,

God-gifted organ-voice of England—

Milton, a name to resound for ages."

I would especially commend to those whom these remarks have interested in any way, the perusal, with a view to this particular object, of "Father Prout's Reliques."

CHAPTER III.

GUIDES AND HANDBOOKS.

The earliest handbook of verse appears to be that of Bysshe, who is, by the way, described in the British Museum Catalogue as "the Poet." The entry is the only ground I can find for so describing him. He is, however, amusingly hard on simple versifiers. "Such Debasers of Rhyme, and Dablers in Poetry would do well to consider that a Man would justly deserve a higher Esteem in the World by being a good Mason or Shoe-Maker, than by being an indifferent or second-Rate Poet." Furthermore, with touching modesty, he says, "I pretend not by the following sheets to teach a man to be a Poet in Spight of Fate and Nature." His "Rules for making English Verse" are reprinted in the Appendix.

His dictionary of rhymes is better than those of his successors,—perhaps I should say "that" of his successors, for Walker's has been repeated with all its errors, or nearly all, in every subsequent handbook. Bysshe is to be praised for setting his face against what Walker styles "allowable" rhymes, such as "haste" and "feast."[7]

Bysshe's theory of verse was "the seat of the accent, and the pause," as distinguished from quantity—that is, it depended on the number of syllables. As a result of this undivided devotion, he misses much of the power to be attained by making the sound the echo of the sense, as Pope puts it. He proposes to alter a line of Dryden's from

> "But forced, harsh, and uneasy unto all."

into

"But forced and harsh, uneasy unto all."

One would fancy the merest tyro would see the intentional harshness of the line as Dryden wrote it, and its utter emasculation as Bysshe reforms it.

Bysshe is strongly in favour of clipping syllables, a very pitiable error, for the chief drawback of English as a poetical language is the preponderance of consonants. He prefers to make "beauteous" dissyllabic, and "victorious" trisyllabic. He recommends the elision which makes "bower," "Heaven," "Prayer" and "higher," monosyllables, and advises the use of such abortions as "temp'rance," "fab'lous," "med'cine," "cov'nant," and even "wall'wing," for wallowing! To compensate for these clippings, however, he considers "ism" a dissyllable!

As a consequence of his narrowing verse to a question of syllable and accent only, he vulgarises many words unnecessarily. The student of verse who considers quantity as well as accent will find no difficulty in reading the following lines without eliding any vowels.

"From diamond quarries hewn, and rocks of gold."—*Milton.*

"A violet by a mossy stone."—*Wordsworth.*

"With vain but violent force their darts they threw."—*Cowley.*

"His ephod, mitre, well-cut diadem on."—*Cowley.*

"My blushing hyacinth and my bays I keep."—*Dryden.*

Bysshe cuts down to "di'mond," "vi'let," "vi'lent," "di'dem," "hy'cinth," words which need no such debasing elision. As in music two short sharp beats are equivalent to one long one (two minims = one semi-breve) so in verse two brief vowels, or syllables even, are admissible—indeed, at times desirable for the sake of variety in lieu of one.

Among less questionable maxims of Bysshe's is one, "avoid a concourse of vowels," instanced by—

"Should th*y I*ambics swell into a book."

This means, it is to be presumed, "avoid a concourse of repetitions of one sound," a very necessary rule. Some poets are careful not to get the same vowel sound twice in any line. "Avoid ending a verse with an adjective whose substantive follows in the next line" is another sound precept, instanced by—

"Some lost their quiet rivals, some their kind

Parents."

The same rule applies to the separation of a preposition from the case which it governs, as exemplified in—

"The daily lessening of our life shows by

A little dying," &c.

With less reason Bysshe condemns alliteration. It is an artifice that can be overdone, as is often the case in Poe's poems, and those of Mr Swinburne,[8]

Following the example of the old *Gradus ad Parnassum*, Bysshe gives an anthology with his guide. An anthology in a guide to English verse is worse than useless, for it serves no purpose save to provoke plagiarism and imitation. Any one who wishes to write verse will do little unless he has a fair acquaintance with English poetry—an acquaintance for which an anthology can never be a substitute; while it will but cripple and hamper his fancy and originality by supplying him with quotations on any given subject, from "April" to "Woman."

Walker's Rhyming Dictionary has greater faults, but also greater merits than Bysshe's Art of Poetry. Walker admits and defends "allowable" rhymes. "It may be objected," he says, "that a work of this kind contributes to extend poetical blemishes, by furnishing imperfect materials and apologies for using them. But it may be answered, that if these imperfect rhymes were allowed to be blemishes, it would still be better to tolerate them than cramp the imagination by the too narrow boundaries of exactly similar sounds." Now, it is perfectly true, of course, that a *poet* may well be allowed to effect the compromise of sacrificing a rhyme for a thought; but the versifier (for whom Walker's book is meant) must have no such license. He must learn to walk before he runs. Yet apart from this, Walker's argument is singularly illogical;—there can be no need to catalogue the blemishes, even on the ground he urges, since the imagination would suggest the license, not the license stimulate the imagination. Walker's book being simply mechanical should have been confined to the correct machinery of verse, and imagination should have been allowed to frame for itself the licenses, which it would not dream of seeking in a handbook.

But for this defect, Walker's Dictionary would be the best book of the sort possible. It contains, beside an Index in which rhymes are arranged under various terminations, as in Bysshe's work, a terminational dictionary of three hundred pages; a dictionary, that is, in which the words are arranged as in ordinary dictionaries, save that the last and not the first letter of the word is that under which it is ranged.

Walker's Index is by no means exhaustive. In arranging the index of this little book I have added about a hundred terminations to his list, beside subdividing headings which have two sounds (as ASH, in "cash" and "wash"). Walker's *Dictionary* of rhymes, though by no means exhaustive, is useful, and is the only one extant. His *Index* of rhymes has been copied so servilely by all compilers of "handbooks of poetry" that, in dismissing it now, we dismiss all so-called rhyming dictionaries of later date.

Of these recent books there are but two of any note or importance. One claims to be a "complete practical guide to the whole subject of English versification"—"an exhaustive treatise," in which the writer, by way of simplifying matters, proposes to supersede the old titles of spondee, dactyl, &c., by the titles of "march," "trip," "quick," and "revert," and makes accents intelligible by calling them "backward" and "forward," with such further lucidities as "hover," "main," "midabout," and other technicalities afford. Its chief characteristic, however, is a decided condemnation of rhyme altogether, and a suggestion of the substitution of "assonance," under which "path" and "ways," and "pride" and "wife" would do duty for rhyme! The treatise, though spoiled by pedantic aiming after novelties of nomenclature, and too assertive language, is worth perusal. But as "a practical guide" it is at present useless, and will remain so until English rhyme is disestablished and disendowed by Act of Parliament. Although its author modestly describes it as "the first treatise of the kind ever completed," and considers it "will in no mean degree serve to advance" the study of English verse, it is to be feared that there is little danger of its setting the Pierian spring on fire.

A more practical "Handbook of Poetry" is the best work of the kind I have met with, but it is full of grave errors. It begins with a definition of "Poetry" which makes it identical with "Verse," and it tends too much to the side of license in consequence, from the fact of permitting to the versifier freedoms which poets only can claim. On rhyme it is singularly inconsistent. It pronounces as no rhyme "heart" and "art," which to any but a cockney ear are perfect rhymes. Yet, a few paragraphs farther on, its only objection to the coupling of "childhood" and "wildwood" as a double rhyme, is that it is hackneyed; whereas it is not a double rhyme at all! In a chapter on "Imagery," though "metaphor" is catalogued, "simile" is omitted, and both together reappear under the needless subdivision "tropes." An anthology is added, and a dictionary of double and treble rhymes—as if it were possible to give anything like an exhaustive list of them in twenty pages!

Such being the imperfections, whether of shortcoming or excess, of the various existing handbooks, I venture to hope that this little treatise may plead some excuse for its appearance.

CHAPTER IV.

OF FEET AND CÆSURA.

The feet most often met with in English verse are those corresponding with the trochee and iambus,[9] that is approximately. The iambic is most common perhaps, represented by two syllables with the accent on the last syllable. The trochee has two syllables, with the accent on the first. An example of a line in each metre will show the difference—

Four Foot Iambic.

"To faí´r Fidé´le's gra´ssy to´mb."

Four Foot Trochaic.

"No´t a si´ngle ma´n depa´rted."

Dactyls (an accented followed by two unaccented syllables) and anapæsts (two unaccented syllables followed by an accented one) are most frequently used in combination with the other feet—

Anapæstic.

"O´r the wo´rld | from the hou´r | of her bi´rth."

Dactylic.

"Ma´ke no deep | scru´tiny

I´nto her | mu´tiny."

It appears to me preferable to retain the classic names for these feet, rather than to try and invent new titles for them. One writer on versification has attempted to do this, and calls the iambic "march" measure, and the trochaic "trip." This seems to me to render the nature of the measure liable to misconstruction, as if the former only suited elevated themes, and the latter light ones; whereas the metre of Hudibras is iambic, and Aytoun's ballad of the "Battle of Flodden" is trochaic. The truth is, that the form of the foot has little to do with the "march" or "trip" of the verse, for "The Bridge of Sighs" is written in a dactylic form; and, according to the authority just alluded to, if the trochee be a "trip," the dactyl must be a "jig"!

By the combinations of these feet in certain numbers a line is constituted. Those in which two, three, and four feet occur—dimeters, trimeters, and tetrameters—are not so general as lines of more feet, and in these latter a new feature has to be recognised and provided for—the cæsura or pause. Strictly, the cæsura causes poetry to be written in lines, the end of each being a cæsura; but there are other cæsuras in the line, one or more according to its length. In the best verse they correspond with a natural pause in the sense of the words. When they do not, the artificial punctuation injures the harmony with which the sound and the sense should flow together. It is by varying the fall of the cæsura that the best writers of blank decasyllabic verse contrive to divest it of monotony. In some of the more irregular forms of verse, especially when it is unrhymed, the cæsura is all-important, giving to the lines their rise and fall—a structure not altogether unlike what has been termed the parallelism of Hebrew versification.

It is scarcely possible to lay down rules for the use of the cæsura, or pause, in English verse. It differs from the classic cæsura in falling at the end of both foot and word. Of its possible varieties we may gain some idea when we note that, in the decassyllabic line, for instance, it may fall after each foot, and it is by the shifting of its place that in this, as in blank verse, monotony is avoided. In shorter measures, especially of a lyric nature, it generally falls midway in the line.

The plan of giving to our accentual feet the titles given to the classical quantitative feet has been strongly condemned by some writers. I venture to think they have hardly considered the matter sufficiently. It must be better to use these meaningless terms (as we use the gibberish of Baroko and Bramantip in logic) than to apply new names which, by aiming at being expressive, may be misleading. But there is something more than this to be considered. There is in accent this, in common with quantity, that just as two shorts make a long, and can be substituted for it, so two unaccented syllables may take the place of one rather more accented; or perhaps it will be found that the substitution is due less to the correspondence in accent alone, than to correspondence of quantity as well as accent. To put it briefly, these resolutions of the foot into more syllables are—like similar resolutions in music—a question of time, and time means quantity rather than accent. As an instance of this, I may give the much-quoted, often-discussed line—

"Than tired eyelids upon tired eyes."

The ordinary method of scanning this is to make a dissyllable of "tired," as if it were "ti-erd," a vulgarism of which its author would never have been guilty. The truth is, that the long "i" and the roll of the "r" correspond in time to a dissyllable, and by changing the run of the line, carry out perfectly Pope's notion of the sound echoing the sense.

These resolutions, therefore, need a most accurate ear, and no slight experience. The versifier will do well, as a beginner, to refrain from attempting them. When he has gone on writing verse by rule of thumb until he begins to discover a formality in them that would be the better for variation, he may fairly try his hand at it—but not until then. Before that, his redundancy of syllables would be the result of faulty or unfinished expression, not the studied cause of a change in run.

CHAPTER V.

METRE AND RHYTHM.

I t was scarcely possible to explain what the feet in verse are without assuming the existence of lines, in order to give intelligible examples of the various feet. But the consideration of the construction of lines really belongs to this chapter.

A line is composed of a certain number of feet, from two to almost any number short of ten or so—if indeed we may limit the number exactly, for there is nothing to prevent a man from writing a line of twenty feet if he have ingenuity enough to maintain the harmony and beat necessary to constitute verse. As a rule, we seldom meet with more than eight feet in a line.

A line may consist of feet of the same description, or of a combination of various feet. And this combination may be exactly repeated in the corresponding line or lines, or one or more of the feet may be replaced by another corresponding in time or quantity. Here is an instance—

"I knew | by the smoke that so gracefully curled ...

And I said | 'if there's peace to be found in the world.'"

Here the iambic "I kne´w" is resolved into the anapæst, "and I sa´id,"[10]—or rather (as the measure is anapæstic) the iambic takes the place of the anapæst.

When only two feet go to a line, it is a dimeter. Three form a trimeter, four a tetrameter, five a pentameter, six a hexameter, seven a heptameter, eight an octameter, which, however, is usually resolved into two tetrameters. If the feet be iambics or trochees, of course the number of syllables will be double that of the feet—thus a pentameter will be decasyllabic. When dactyls or anapæsts are used, of course the number of syllables exceeds the double of the feet. But there is no necessity for enlarging on this point: I have given enough to explain terms, with which the student may perhaps meet while reading up the subject of versification. As he may also meet with the terms "catalectic" and "acatalectic," it may be as well to give a brief explanation of them also. A catalectic line is one in which the last foot is not completed. An acatalectic is one in which the line and the foot terminate together. An extract from the "Bridge of Sighs," a dactylic poem, will illustrate this.

"Make no deep | scrutiny
Into her | mutiny;
Rash and un | dutiful,
Past all dis | honour;
Death has left | on her
Only the | beautiful.

Take her up | tenderly,
Lift her with | care;
Fashion'd so | slenderly
Young and so | fair."

Here the fourth and fifth, the eighth and tenth lines are catalectic. In the first two the last foot needs one syllable, in the others it requires two. It is scarcely necessary to point out how such variations improve and invigorate the measure, by checking the gallop of the verse.

We have now seen that the line may be composed of various numbers of the different feet. The next step to consider is the combination of lines into stanzas.

Stanzas are formed of two or more lines. Two lines are styled a couplet, three a triplet, and four a quatrain, while other combinations owe their titles to those who have used them first or most, as in the case of the Spenserian stanza.

The reader will see at once that, each of these kinds of stanzas being constructible of any of the styles of line before enumerated, each style of line being in its turn constructible of any of the sorts of feet described in a previous chapter, to make any attempt to give an exhaustive list of stanzas would be to enter upon an arithmetical progression alarming to think of.[11] I shall therefore only enumerate a few, giving, as seems most useful for my purpose, examples of the most common form of a peculiar stanza, as in the case of the decasyllabic couplet of Pope, and the nine-line stanza of Spenser, or the least common, as when, in the quatrain, it appears preferable to give, instead of the alternate-rhymed octosyllabic tetrameters which have been repeated *ad nauseam*, such fresh forms as will be found in the extracts from "The Haunted House," or Browning's "Pretty Woman."

EXAMPLES.

THE COUPLET OR DISTICH.[12]

Dimeter (four-syllabled).

"Here, here I live
And somewhat give."

—*Herrick, Hesperides.*

Tetrameter (eight-syllabled).

"His tawny beard was th' equal grace
Both of his wisdom and his face."

—*Butler, Hudibras.*

Tetrameter (seven-syllabled).

"As it fell upon a day
In the merry month of May."

—*Shakespeare.*

Pentameter (ten-syllabled, "Pope's decasyllable").

"Truth from his lips prevail'd with double sway,
And fools who came to scoff remained to pray."

—*Goldsmith, Deserted Village.*

Hexameter (twelve-syllabled).

"Doth beat the brooks and ponds for sweet refreshing soil:
That serving not—then proves if he his scent may foil."

—*Drayton, Polyolbion.*

Heptameter (fourteen-syllabled).

"Now glory to the Lord of Hosts, from whom all glories are;
And glory to our sovereign liege, king Henry of Navarre."

—*Macaulay, Battle of Ivry.*

The couplet may also be formed of two lines of irregular length.

"Belovëd, O men's mother, O men's queen!
Arise, appear, be seen."

—Swinburne, Ode to Italy.

"Where the quiet-coloured end of evening smiles
Miles on miles."

—Browning, Love among the Ruins.

"Morning, evening, noon, and night,
'Praise God,' sang Theocrite."

—Browning, The Boy and the Angel.

"Take the cloak from his face and at first
Let the corpse do its worst."

—Browning, After.

"Or for a time we'll lie
As robes laid by."

—Herrick, Hesperides.

"Give me a cell
To dwell."

—Herrick, Hesperides.

Two couplets are at times linked together into a quatrain. More often they are formed into six-line stanzas, that is a couplet followed by a line which has its rhyme in another line following the second couplet. But indeed the combination of stanzas is almost inexhaustible.

TRIPLETS.

Trimeter (six-syllabled).

"And teach me how to sing
Unto the lyric string
My measures ravishing."

—Herrick, Hesperides.

Tetrameter (seven-syllabled).

"O, thou child of many prayers,

Life hath quicksands, life hath snares,

Care and age come unawares."

—Longfellow, Maidenhood.

Octameter (fifteen syllabled).

"Was a lady such a lady, cheeks so round and lips so red—

On her neck the small face buoyant, like a bell-flower o'er its bed,

O'er the breast's superb abundance where a man might base his head."

—Browning, A Toccata.

The triplet pure and simple, is not a very common form; it is most frequently combined with other forms to make longer stanzas. At times the second line, instead of rhyming with the first or third, finds an echo in the next triplet—sometimes in the second, but more often in the first and third lines.

"Make me a face on the window there,

Waiting, as ever mute the while,

My love to pass below in the square.

And let me think that it may beguile

Dreary days, which the dead must spend

Down in their darkness under the aisle."

—Browning, The Statue and the Bust.

Another species of triplet occurs in the Pope measure (pentameter-decasyllabic). It is formed by the introduction, after an ordinary couplet, of a third line, repeating the rhyme and consisting of eleven syllables and six feet. Dryden, however, and some other writers, gave an occasional triplet without the extra foot. The Alexandrine, *i.e.*, the six-foot line, ought to close the sense, and conclude with a full stop.

THE QUATRAIN.

Of this form of stanza the name is legion. Of the most common styles, the reader's memory will supply numerous examples. I shall merely give a few of the rarer kinds. The quatrain may consist practically of two couplets, or of a couplet divided by a couplet, as in Tennyson's "In Memoriam." But the usual rule is to rhyme the first and third, and second and fourth. The laxity which leaves the two former unrhymed, is a practice which cannot be too strongly condemned. Quatrains so formed should in honesty be written as couplets, but such a condensation would possibly not suit the views of the mob of magazine-versifiers, who have inflicted this injury, with many others, upon English versification.

It may be well to note here that the rhyme of the first and third lines should be as dissimilar as possible in sound to that of the second and fourth. This is, in fact, a part of the rule which forbids repetitions of the same vowel-sounds in a line—chief of all, a repetition of the particular vowel-sound of the rhyme. The rhymes recurring give a beat which is something like a cæsura, and when therefore the rhyme-sound occurs elsewhere than at its correct post it mars the flow. Here follow a few examples of the quatrain. I have not specified the syllables or feet, as the reader by this time will have learned to scan for himself; and, owing to the varieties of measure, such a specification would be cumbrous:—

"The woodlouse dropp'd and roll'd into a ball,

Touch'd by some impulse, occult or mechanic,

And nameless beetles ran along the wall

In universal panic."

—*Hood, Haunted House.*

"That fawn-skin-dappled hair of hers,

And the blue eye,

Dear and dewy,

And that infantine fresh air of hers."

—*Browning, A Fair Woman.*

"All thoughts, all passions, all delights,

Whatever stirs this mortal frame;

All are but ministers of love,

And feed his sacred flame."

—*Coleridge, Love.*

"What constitutes a state?

Not high-raised battlement or labour'd mound,

Thick wall, or moated gate,

Nor cities proud with spires and turrets crown'd."

—*Jones, Ode.*

"Whither, midst falling dew,

While glow the heavens with the last steps of day,

Far through their rosy depths, dost thou pursue

Thy solitary way."

—*Bryant, To a Waterfowl.*

"Sweet day, so calm, so cool, so bright,

The bridal of the earth and sky,

The dews shall weep thy fall to-night,

For thou must die."

—*Herbert, Virtue.*

THE FIVE-LINE STANZA.

I am inclined to think this one of the most musical forms of the stanza we possess. It is capable of almost endless variety, and the proportions of rhymes, three and two, seem to be especially conducive to harmony. It would be curious to go into the question how many popular poems are in this form. Here are two examples—both of them from favourite pieces:—

"Go, lovely rose,

Tell her that wastes her time and me,

That now she knows

When I resemble her to thee,

How sweet and fair she seems to be."

—*Waller, To a Rose.*

"Higher still and higher

From the earth thou springest;

Like a cloud of fire,

The blue deep thou wingest,

And singing still dost soar, and soaring ever singest."

Mr Browning frequently uses this stanza, and with admirable effect. Although he has been accused of ruggedness by some critics, there is no modern poet who has a greater acquaintance with the various forms of verse, or can handle them more ably. The following are examples of his treatment:—

"Is it your moral of life?

Such a web, simple and subtle,

Weave we on earth here, in impotent strife

Backward and forward each throwing his shuttle—

Death ending all with a knife?"

—*Master Hugues.*

"And yonder at foot of the fronting ridge,

That takes the turn to a range beyond,

Is the chapel, reach'd by the one-arch'd bridge,

Where the water is stopp'd in a stagnant pond,

Danced over by the midge."

—*By the Fireside.*

"Stand still, true poet that you are!

I know you; let me try and draw you.

Some night you'll fail us; when afar

You rise, remember one man saw you—

Knew you—and named a star,"

—*Popularity.*

"Not a twinkle from the fly,

Not a glimmer from the worm.

When the crickets stopp'd their cry,

When the owls forbore a term,

You heard music—that was I!"

—A Serenade.

"When the spider to serve his ends,

By a sudden thread,

Arms and legs outspread,

On the table's midst descends—

Comes to find God knows what friends!"

—Mesmerism.

THE SIX-LINE STANZA.

With the increasing number of lines comes an increasing number of combinations of rhymes. There is the combination of three couplets, and there is that of two couplets, with another pair of rhymes one line after the first, the other after the second couplet. Then there is a quatrain of alternate rhymes, and a final couplet—to mention no others.

"Fear no more the heat o' the sun,

Nor the furious winter's rages;

Thou thy worldly task hast done.

Home art gone, and ta'en thy wages—

Golden lads and girls all must

Like chimney-sweepers come to dust."

—Shakespeare.

"One day, it matters not to know

How many hundred years ago,

A Spaniard stopt at a posada door;

The landlord came to welcome him and chat

Of this and that,

For he had seen the traveller here before."

—*Southey, St Romuald.*

"And wash'd by my cosmetic brush,
How Beauty's cheeks began to blush
With locks of auburn stain—
Not Goldsmith's Auburn, nut-brown hair
That made her loveliest of the fair,
Not loveliest of the plain."

—*Hood, Progress of Art.*

"Some watch, some call, some see her head emerge
Wherever a brown weed falls through the foam;
Some point to white eruptions of the surge—
But she is vanish'd to her shady home,
Under the deep inscrutable, and there
Weeps in a midnight made of her own hair."

—*Hood, Hero and Leander.*

"Ever drifting, drifting, drifting,
On the shifting
Currents of the restless heart—
Till at length in books recorded,
They like hoarded
Household words no more depart."

—*Longfellow, Seaweed.*

"Before me rose an avenue
Of tall and sombrous pines;
Abroad their fanlike branches grew,
And where the sunshine darted through,
Spread a vapour, soft and blue,

In long and sloping lines."

—*Longfellow, Prelude.*

The following form may be looked upon as Burns's exclusively:—

"Wee, modest, crimson-tipped flower,—

Thou'st met me in an evil hour,

For I maun crush among the stour

Thy slender stem;

To spare thee now is past my power,

Thou bonnie gem."

—*To a Mountain Daisy.*

THE SEVEN-LINE STANZA.

This form is not very common. It may be formed of a quatrain and triplet; of a quatrain, a line rhyming the last of the quatrain, and a couplet; of a quatrain, a couplet, and a line rhyming the fourth line. Or these may be reversed.

THE EIGHT-LINE STANZA.

This is susceptible of endless variety, commencing with two quatrains, or a six-line stanza and a couplet, or two triplets with a brace of rhyming lines, one after each triplet.

"Thus lived—thus died she; nevermore on her

Shall sorrow light or shame. She was not made

Through years or moons the inner weight to bear,

Which colder hearts endure till they are laid

By age in earth; her days and pleasures were

Brief but delightful; such as had not staid

Long with her destiny. But she sleeps well

By the sea-shore whereon she loved to dwell."

—*Byron, Don Juan.*

THE NINE-LINE STANZA.

Of this form the most generally used is the Spenserian, or the following variation of it:—

"A little, sorrowful, deserted thing,

Begot of love and yet no love begetting;

Guiltless of shame, and yet for shame to wring;

And too soon banish'd from a mother's petting

To churlish nature and the wide world's fretting,

For alien pity and unnatural care;

Alas! to see how the cold dew kept wetting

His childish coats, and dabbled all his hair

Like gossamers across his forehead fair."

—*Hood, Midsummer Fairies.*

The Spenserian has the same arrangement of the rhymes, but has an extra foot in the last line. The two last lines of a stanza from "Childe Harold" will illustrate this:—

"To mingle with the universe and feel

What I can ne'er express, yet cannot all conceal."

—*Byron.*

The formation of the ten, eleven, twelve, &c., line stanzas is but an adaptation of those already described. A single fourteen-line stanza of a certain arrangement of rhyme is a sonnet, but as the sonnet is scarcely versifiers' work, I will not occupy space by the lengthy explanation it would require. On the same grounds, I am almost inclined to omit discussion of blank verse, but will give a brief summary of its varieties. The ordinary form of blank verse is the decasyllabic in which Milton's "Paradise Lost" is written—

"Of man's first disobedience and the fruit

Of that forbidden tree whose mortal taste

Brought death into the world and all our woe."

This consists of ten syllables with an accented following an unaccented syllable. It is preserved from monotony by the varying fall of the cæsura or pause. It occurs but rarely after the first foot or the eighth foot, and not often after the third and seventh. Elisions and the substitution of a trisyllable, equivalent in time for a dissyllable, are met with, and at times the accent is shifted, when by the change the sense of the line gains in vigour of expression, as in—

"Once found, which yet unfound, most would have thought

Impossible."

According to scansion "most wo'uld," but by the throwing back of the accent strengthened and distinguished into "*most* would have thought." [In addition to this in the blank verse of the stage, we find occasionally additional syllables, as—

"Or to take arms against a sea of troub(les)."]

Other forms of blank verse follow:—

1. "If aught of oaten stop or pastoral song

May hope, chaste Eve, to soothe thy modest ear,

Like thy own solemn springs,

Thy springs and dying gales."

—*Collins, Ode to Evening.*

2. "But never could I tune my reed

At morn, or noon, or eve, so sweet,

As when upon the ocean shore

I hail'd thy star-beam mild."

—*Kirke White, Shipwrecked Solitary's Song.*

3. "Who at this untimely hour

Wanders o'er the desert sands?

No station is in view,

No palm-grove islanded amidst the waste,—

The mother and her child,

The widow'd mother and the fatherless boy,

They at this untimely hour

Wander o'er the desert sands."[13]

—*Southey, Thalaba.*

4. "Friend of my bosom, thou more than a brother,

Why wast not thou born in my father's dwelling?

So might we talk of the old familiar faces."

—*Lamb.*

5. "See how he scorns all human arguments

So that no oar he wants, nor other sail

Than his own wings between so distant shores."[14]

—*Longfellow, Translation of Dante.*

6. "Yet dost thou recall

Days departed, half-forgotten,

When in dreamy youth I wander'd

By the Baltic."

—*Longfellow, To a Danish Song-Book.*

7. "All things in earth and air

Bound were by magic spell

Never to do him harm;

Even the plants and stones,

All save the mistletoe,

The sacred mistletoe."

—*Longfellow, Tegner's Drapa.*

8. "Give me of your bark, O birch-tree!

Of your yellow bark, O birch-tree!

Growing by the rushing river,

Tall and stately in the valley."

—*Longfellow, Hiawatha.*

9. "Heard he that cry of pain; and through the hush that succeeded

Whisper'd a gentle voice, in accents tender and saintlike,

'Gabriel, oh, my beloved!' and died away into silence."

—Longfellow, Evangeline.

An extremely musical form of blank verse, the trochaic, will be found in Browning's "One Word More":—

"I shall never in the years remaining,

Paint you pictures, no, nor carve you statues,

Make you music that should all-express me;

So it seems; I stand on my attainment:

This of verse alone one life allows me;

Verse and nothing else have I to give you.

Other heights in other loves, God willing—

All the gifts from all the heights, your own, love!"

This by no means exhausts the varieties of blank verse; but, as I have already said, blank verse is, on the whole, scarcely to be commended to the student for practice, because it is, while apparently the easiest, in reality the most difficult form he could attempt. It is in fact particularly easy to attain the blankness—but the verse is another matter. The absence of rhymes necessitates the most perfect melody and harmony, if the lines are to be anything beyond prose chopped up into lengths.

There are, I should mention before closing this chapter, many more styles of stanza than I have named, and many varieties of them. The ode is of somewhat irregular construction, but like the sonnet it is, I consider, beyond the scope of those for whom this book is intended, and it needs not to be discussed on that account.

CHAPTER VI.

OF RHYME.

A rhyme must commence on an accented syllable. From the accented vowel of that syllable to the end, the two or more words intended to rhyme must be identical in sound; but the letters preceding the accented vowel must in each case be dissimilar in sound. Thus "learn," "fern," "discern," are rhymes, with the common sound of "ern" preceded by the dissimilar sounds of "l," "f," "sc." "Possess" and "recess" do not rhyme, having besides the common "ess" the similar pronunciation of the "c" and the double "s" preceding it. The letters "r" and "l," when preceded by other consonants, so as practically to form new letters, can be rhymed to the simple "r" and "l" respectively, thus "track" and "rack," "blame" and "lame," are rhymes. The same rule applies to letters preceded by "s," "smile" being a rhyme to "mile." Similarly "h" and its compound rhyme, *e.g.*, "shows," "those," "chose," and any word ending in "phose" with "hose."

The aspirate to any but a Cockney would of course pass as constituting the needful difference at the beginning of a rhyme, as in "heart" and "art," "hair" and "air."[15]

In the case of "world" and "whirl'd," however, I fear common usage must compel us to declare against the rhyme, since the practice of pronouncing the "h" after "w" is daily becoming more and more uncommon.

Rhymes are single, double, or treble—or more properly one-syllabled, two-syllabled, and three-syllabled. Rhymes of four or more syllables are peculiar to burlesque or comic verse. Indeed, Dryden declared that only one-syllabled rhymes were suitable for grave subjects: but every one must have at his fingers' ends scores of proofs to the contrary, of which I will instance but one—"The Bridge of Sighs."

Monosyllables or polysyllables accented on the last syllable are "single" rhymes. Words accented on the penultimate or last syllable but one supply "double" rhymes; *e.g.*, agita´ted, ela´ted. When the accent is thrown another syllable back, and falls on the antepenultimate as in "a´rrogate," it is in the first place a "triple" rhyme. But as in English there is a tendency to alternate the acute and grave accent, the trisyllable has practically two rhymes, a three-syllabled and a one-syllabled—thus "arrogate" and "Harrogate" rhyme, but "arrogate" may also pair off with "mate." Nevertheless it is necessary to be cautious in the use of words with this spurious accent—it is perhaps better still to avoid them. Such words as "merrily," "beautiful," "purity," ought never to be used as single-syllabled rhymes:—even such words as "merited" and "happiness" have a forced sound when so used.

Elisions should be avoided, though "bow'r" and "flow'r" may pass muster, with some others. "Ta'en," "e'er," "e'en," and such contractions may of course be used. The articles, prepositions, and such, cannot in serious verse stand as rhymes, under the same rule which condemns the separation of the adjective from its substantive in the next line.

It is scarcely necessary to premise that to write verse decently the student must have a thorough knowledge of grammar. From ignorance on that score arise naturally blemishes enough to destroy verse, as they would poetry, almost. I have seen verses which, beginning by apostrophising some one as "thou," slipped in a few lines into "yours" and "you"—or, worse still, have said "thou doeth," or "thou, who is."

Expletives and mean expressions also must be excluded. The verse should never soar to "high-falutin," or sink to commonplace language. Simplicity is not commonplace, and nobility is not "high-falutin," and they should be aimed at accordingly;—when you have acquired the one, you will as a rule find the other in its company.

When three or more lines are intended to rhyme together, the common base or accented vowel in each instance must be preceded by a different sound. For example "born," "corn," and "borne," will not serve for a triplet, because, though the first and third are both rhymes to the second, they are not rhymes to each other.

It is as well, unless you are thoroughly acquainted with the pronunciation of foreign languages, to abstain from using them in verse, especially in rhymes. I met with the following instance of the folly of such rhyming in a magazine, not long ago—

"Prim Monsieurs fresh from Boulogne's *Bois*...

For these the Row's a certain *draw*."

This is about as elegant as rhyming "Boulogne" and "Song."

It is wise—on the principle of rhyme, the difference of sounds preceding the common base—to avoid any similarity by combination. For example, "is" is a good rhyme for "'tis," but you should be careful not to let "it" immediately precede the "is," as it mars the necessary dissimilarity of the opening sound of the two rhymes.

Let the beginner remember one thing:—rhyme is a fetter, undoubtedly. Let him therefore refrain from attempting measures with frequent rhymes, for experience alone can give ease in such essays. Only the skilled can dance gracefully in fetters. Moreover, a too frequent repetition of rhyme at short intervals gives a jigginess to the verse. It is on this account that the use in a line of a sound similar to the rhyme should be avoided.[16]

As a final warning, let me entreat the writer of verses to examine his rhymes carefully, and see that they chime to an educated ear. Such atrocities as "morn" and "dawn," "more" and "sure," "light in" and "writing," "fought" and "sort," are fatal to the success of verse. They stamp it with vulgarity, as surely as the dropping of the "h" stamps a speaker. Furthermore, do not make a trisyllable of a dissyllable—as, for instance, by pronouncing "ticklish" "tick-el-ish," and if you have cause to rhyme "iron," try "environ" or "Byron," not "my urn," because only the vulgar pronounce it "iern," or "apron" "apern," &c.

CHAPTER VII.

OF FIGURES.

The figures most commonly used in verse are similes and metaphors. A simile is a figure whereby one thing is likened to another. It is ushered in by a "like" or an "as."

"Like sportive deer they coursed about"

—*Hood, Eugene Aram.*

"Such a brow

His eyes had to live under, clear as flint."

—*Browning, A Contemporary.*

"Resembles sorrow only

As the mist resembles rain."

—*Longfellow, The Day is Done.*

"Look how a man is lower'd to his grave ...

So is he sunk into the yawning wave."

—*Hood, Hero and Leander.*

A metaphor is a figure whereby the one thing, instead of being likened to the other, is, as it were, transformed into it, and is described as doing what it (the other) does.

"Poetry is

The grandest chariot wherein king-thoughts ride."

—*Smith, Life Drama.*

"The anchor, whose giant hand

Would reach down and grapple with the land."

—*Longfellow, Building of the Ship.*

Sometimes the two are united in one passage, as in—

"The darkness

Falls from the wings of night,

As a feather is wafted downward."

—Longfellow, *The Day is Done.*

The last line is a simile, but "the wings of night" is metaphorical. "A simile," says Johnson, "to be perfect, must both illustrate and ennoble the subject; but either of these qualities may be sufficient to recommend it."

Alliteration, when not overdone, is an exquisite addition to the charm of verse. The Poet Laureate thoroughly understands its value. Mr Swinburne allows it too frequently to run riot. Edgar Allan Poe carried it to extravagance. I select an example from each:—

"The moan of doves in immemorial elms,

And murmur of innumerable bees."

—*Tennyson.*

"The lilies and languors of virtue,

For the raptures and roses of vice."

—*Swinburne, Dolores.*

"Come up through the lair of the lion

With love in her luminous eyes."

—*Poe, Ulalume.*

The instance from the Poet Laureate is a strong one—the repetition of the "m" is to express the sound of the bees and the elms. The alternation in the others is only pleasing to the ear, and the artifice in the last instance certainly is too obvious. In the Poet Laureate's lines the alliteration is so ingeniously contrived that one scarcely would suppose there are as many as seven repetitions of the "m." In Poe's, one is surprised to find the apparent excess of alliteration is due to but four repetitions. But the "l's" are identical with the strongest beats in the line, whereas the "m's" in Tennyson's line are interspersed with other letters at the beats. He uses this artifice more frequently than those would suspect who have not closely examined his poems, for he thoroughly appreciates the truth of the maxim, *ars est celare artem.* A few lines from "The Princess" will illustrate this:—

"The baby that by us,

Half-lapt in glowing gauze and golden brede,

Lay like a new-fall'n meteor on the grass,

Uncared-for, spied its mother and began

A blind and babbling laughter, and to dance

Its body, and reach its falling innocent arms

And lazy ling'ring fingers."

Here a careful study will reveal alliteration within alliteration, and yet the effect is perfect, for there is no sign of labour.

Under this category may come, I think, a description of the Rondeau—a poem of which the first few words are repeated at the end. It was at one time ruled to be of a certain number of lines, but the restriction scarcely holds good now. The best rondeau in the language is Leigh Hunt's:—

"Jenny kiss'd me when we met,

Jumping from the chair she sat in;

Time, you thief, who love to get

Sweets upon your list, put that in!

Say I'm weary, say I'm sad;

Say that health and wealth have miss'd me;

Say I'm growing old, but add—

Jenny kiss'd me!"

Elision must be used with a sparing hand. Generally speaking, a vowel that is so slightly pronounced that it can be elided, as in "temperance"—"temp'rance," may just as well be left in, and accounted for by managing to get the "quantity" to cover it. Where it is too strongly pronounced, to cut it out is to disfigure and injure the line, as in the substitution of "wall'wing" for "wallowing." That elision is often used unnecessarily may be seen in the frequency with which, in reading verse, we—according to most authorities—elide the "y" of "many"—

"Full many a flower is doom'd to blush unseen."

—Gray.

Here we are told we elide the "y" of "many," and some would replace "flower" by "flow'r." Yet to the most sensitive ear these may receive, in reading, their share of pronunciation, without damage to the flow of the line, if the reader understands quantity. "To" is often similarly "elided," as in—

"Can he to a friend—to a son so bloody grow?"

—Cowley.

On the other hand, it is as well not to make too frequent use of the accented "ed," as in "amazéd." In "belovéd" and a few more words it is commonly used, and does not, therefore, sound strange. In others it gives a forced and botched air to the verse.

In verse some latitude is allowed in arranging the order of words in a sentence, but it must not be indulged in too freely. A study of the style of our best poets is the only means of learning what is allowable and what is not; it is impossible to explain it within the limits of this treatise. It may, however, be laid down, as a first principle, that no change in the order of words is admissible, if it gives rise to any doubt as to their real meaning:— for example, if you wish to say, "the dog bit the cat," although such an inversion of construction as putting the objective before, and the nominative after, the verb, is allowed in verse, it is scarcely advisable to adopt it, and say, "the cat bit the dog."

CHAPTER VIII.

OF BURLESQUE AND COMIC VERSE, AND *VERS DE SOCIÉTÉ.*

I t will be as well for the reader to divest himself at once of the notion that verse of this class is the lowest and easiest form he can essay, or that the rules which govern it are more lax than those which sway serious composition. The exact contrary is the case. Comic or burlesque verse is ordinary verse *plus* something. Ordinary verse may pass muster if its manner be finished, but comic verse must have some matter as well. Yet it does not on that account claim any license in rhyme, for it lacks the gravity and importance of theme which may at times, in serious poetry, be pleaded as outweighing a faulty rhyme.

This style of writing needs skill in devising novel and startling turns of rhyme, rhythm, or construction, and can hardly be employed by those who do not possess some articulate wit or humour—that is to say, the power of expressing, not merely of appreciating, those qualities.

A defective rhyme is a fault in serious verse—it is a crime in comic. It is no sin to be ignorant of Greek or Latin, but it is worse than a blunder, under such circumstances, to quote them—and quote them incorrectly. In the same way, one is not compelled to write comic verse, but if he does write it, and cannot do so correctly, he deserves severe handling.

One of the leading characteristics of this style is dexterous rhyming—and the legerdemain must be effected with genuine coin, not dumps. In the very degree that clever composite rhyming assists in making the verse sparkling and effective, it must bear the closest scrutiny and analysation—must be real Moet, not gooseberry.

All, then, that has been said with regard to serious verse applies with double force to the lighter form of *vers de société.* According to the definition of Mr Frederick Locker, no mean authority, *vers de société* should be "short, elegant, refined, and fanciful, not seldom distinguished by chastened sentiment, and often playful. The tone should not be pitched high; it should be idiomatic, and rather in the conversational key; the rhythm should be crisp and sparkling, and the rhyme frequent, and never forced, while the entire poem should be marked by tasteful moderation, high finish, and completeness: *for however trivial the subject-matter may be,—indeed, rather in proportion to its triviality,—subordination to the rules of composition, and perfection of execution, should be strictly enforced.*"

Let me entreat the reader to bear that italicised sentence in memory when writing any style of verse, but most especially when he essays the comic or burlesque.

No precedent for laxity can be pleaded because the poets who have at times indulged in such trifling, have therein availed themselves of the licenses which they originally took out for loftier writing. *Non semper arcum tendit Apollo*, and the poet may be excused for striking his lyre with careless fingers. But we, who do not pretend to possess lyres, must be careful about the fingering of our kits. Apollo's slackened bow offers no precedent for the popgun of the poetaster.

As I have already said, much of the merit of this style depends on the scintillations, so to speak, of its rhymes. They must therefore be perfect. When Butler wrote the much-quoted couplet:—

"When pulpit, drum ecclesiastick,

Was beat with fist instead of a stick."

he was guilty of coupling "astick" and "a stick" together as a rhyme, which they do not constitute. But he who on that account claims privilege to commit a similar offence, not only is guilty of the vanity of demanding to be judged on the same level as Butler, but is illogical. Two wrongs cannot constitute a right, and all the bad rhyming in the world can be no extenuation of a repetition of the offence.

The results of carelessness in such matters are but too apparent! The slipshod that has been for so long suffered to pass for comic verse, has brought the art into disrepute. In the case of burlesque, this is even more plainly discernible. It is held in so small esteem, that people have come to forget that it boasts Aristophanes as its founder! Halting measures, cockney rhymes, and mere play on sound, instead of sense, in punning, have gone near to being the death of what at its worst was an amusing pastime, at its best was healthy satire.

The purchase of half-a-dozen modern burlesques at Mr Lacy's, will account for the declining popularity of burlesque. *All* of them will be found defaced by defective rhymes, and cockneyisms too common to provoke a smile. In the majority of them the decasyllabic metre will be found to range from six or eight syllables to twelve or fourteen! Most bear the same relation to real burlesque-writing, that the schoolboy's picture of his master—a circle for head and four scratches for arms and legs—bears to genuine caricature.

The most telling form of rhyme in comic versification is the polysyllabic, and the greater the number of assonant syllables in such rhymes the more effective they prove. The excellence is co-extensive, however, with the unexpectedness and novelty, and there is therefore but small merit in such a polysyllabic rhyme as—

"From Scotland's mountains down he came,

And straightway up to town he came."

This merely consists of the single rhymes "down" and "town," with "he came" as a common affix. Such polysyllables may be admitted here and there in a long piece, but when they constitute the whole or even a majority of the rhymes, the writer is imposing on his readers. He is swelling his balance at his banker's by adding noughts on the right hand of the pounds' figure without paying in the cash.

Another feature of this style of verse is the repetition of rhymes. Open the "Ingoldsby Legends,"[17] which may be taken as the foundation of one school of comic verse, and you will scarcely fail to light upon a succession of rhymes, coming one after the other, like a string of boys at leap-frog, as if the well-spring of rhyme were inexhaustible.

Although punning scarcely comes within the scope of this treatise, it may not be amiss to remind those who may desire to essay comic verse, that a pun is a double-*meaning*. It is not sufficient to get two words that clink alike, or to torture by mispronunciation a resemblance in sound between words or combinations of words. There must be an echo in the sense—"a likeness in unlikeness" in the idea.

Proper names should not be used as rhymes. The only exception is in the case of any real individual of note—a statesman, author, or actor, when to find a telling rhyme to the name, a rhyme suggestive of the habits or pursuits of the owner of that name, has some merit, especially if the name be long and peculiar. But to introduce an imaginary name for the sake of a rhyme, is work that is too cheap to be good. A child can write such rhyme as—

"A man of strict veracity

Was Peter James M'Assity."

In composite rhyming the greatest care should be taken to see that each syllable after the first is identical in sound in each line. In "use he was" and "juicy was," the "h" destroys the rhyme, and the difference in sound in the last syllable (however carelessly pronounced) between such words as "oakum" and "smoke 'em" has a similar disqualifying power. It is scarcely necessary to refer to such inadmissible couples as "protector" and "neglect her," "birching" and "urchin," "oracle" and "historical."

One trick in rhyming is often very effective, but it must not be put into force too often. In some instances, however, it tells with great comical effect, by affording a rhyme to a word which at first glance the reader thinks it is impossible to rhyme. Canning, in the "Anti-Jacobin," used it with ludicrous effect in Rogero's song, and a few lines from that will illustrate and explain the trick I allude to:—

"Here doom'd to starve on water gru-

-el, never shall I see the U-

-niversity of Gottingen!"

Here the division of the words "gruel" and "University" has an extremely absurd effect. But the artifice must be used sparingly, and those who employ it must beware of one pitfall. The moiety of the word which is carried over to begin the next line must be considered as a fresh word occupying the first foot. There is a tendency to overlook it, and count it as part of the previous line, and that of course is a fatal error.

Parody may be considered as a form of comic versification. It is not enough that a parody should be in the same metre as the original poem it imitates. Nor is it sufficient that the first line or so has such a similarity as to suggest the original. In the best parodies each line of the original has an echo in the parody, and the words of the former are retained as far as possible in the latter, or replaced by others very similar.

Another form of parody is the parody of style, when, instead of selecting a particular poem to paraphrase, we imitate, in verse modelled on the form he usually adopts, the mannerisms of thought or expression for which any particular writer is distinguished.

Examples of both kinds of parody will be found in the "Rejected Addresses" of James and Horace Smith, which should be studied together with Hood, Barham, Wolcot, and Thackeray, by those who would read the best models of humorous, comic, or burlesque writing. I may add here that *vers de société* will be best studied in the writings of Praed, Prior, and Moore. From living writers it would be invidious to single out any, either as models or warnings.

CHAPTER IX.

OF SONG-WRITING.

Although song-writing is one of the most difficult styles of versification, it is now held in but little repute, owing to the unfortunate condition of the musical world in England. "Any rubbish will do for music" is the maxim of the music-shopkeeper, who is practically the arbiter of the art now-a-days, and who has the interests, he is supposed to represent, so little at heart that he would not scruple to publish songs, consisting of "nonsense verses"—as schoolboys call them,—set to music, if he thought that the usual artifice of paying singers a royalty on the sale for singing a song would prevail on the public to buy them.

Another reason why "any rubbish will do for music" has passed into a proverb is, that few amateur singers—and not too many professionals—understand "phrasing." How rarely can one hear what the words of a song are! Go to a "musical evening" and take note, and you will see that, in nine cases out of ten, when a new song has been sung, people take the piece of music and look over the words. A song is like a cherry, and ought not to require us to make two bites at it.

Nor is the injury inflicted on music due only to the amount of rubbish which is made to do duty for songs. The writings of our poets are ransacked for "words," and accompaniments are manufactured to poems which were never intended, and are absolutely unfitted, for musical treatment. Then, because it is found that poems are not to be converted into songs so easily as people think, the cry is not merely that "any rubbish will do for songs," but that "*only* rubbish will do,"—a cry that is vigorously taken up by interested persons.

The truth lies between the two extremes. A peculiar style of verse is required, marked by such characteristics, and so difficult of attainment, that some of our greatest poets—Byron for one—have failed as song-writers. English literature reckons but few really good song-writers. When you have named Moore, Lover, Burns, and Barry Cornwall, you have almost exhausted the list.

There is in the last edition of the works of the lamented writer I have just named—Samuel Lover—a preface in which he enters very minutely into the subject of song-writing. The sum of what he says is, that "the song being necessarily of brief compass, the writer must have powers of condensation. He must possess ingenuity in the management of metre. He must frame it of open vowels, with as few guttural or hissing sounds as possible, and he must be content sometimes to sacrifice grandeur or vigour to the necessity of selecting *singing* words and not *reading* ones." He adds that "the simplest words best suit song, but simplicity must not descend to baldness. There must be a thought in the song, gracefully expressed, and it must appeal either to the fancy or feelings, or both, but rather by suggestion than direct appeal; and philosophy and didactics must be eschewed."

He adduces Shelley, with his intense poetry and exquisite sensitiveness to sweet sounds, as an instance of a poet who failed to see the exact necessities of song-writing, and gives a quotation from one of Shelley's "songs" to prove this. The line is—

"The fresh earth in new leaves drest."

and he says very pertinently, "It is a sweet line, and a pleasant image—but I defy any one to sing it: *nearly every word shuts up the mouth instead of opening it.*" That last sentence is the key to song-writing. I use the word song-writing in preference to "lyrical writing," because "lyrical" has been warped from its strict meaning, and applied to verse which was not intended for music. It is not absolutely necessary that a song-writer should have a practical knowledge of music, but it is all the better if he have: beyond doubt, Moore owed much of his success to his possession of musical knowledge.

DICTIONARY OF RHYMES.

Explanation of Signs, etc.

† Words obsolete, antiquated, and rare.

* Provincialisms, or local terms.

§ Slang, vulgar, or commonplace words.

¶ Technical or unusual words.

| | Foreign words, naturalised to some extent.

N.B.—When under one termination other spellings occur,—*e.g.*, under IRM, *term* and *worm*,—the reader should refer to them; *i.e.*, ERM and ORM.

A.

There is an uncertainty, and therefore a choice, as to the pronunciation of many words ending in "a." Most are of classical or foreign derivation, and hence may come under A1, or A2; or perhaps even under a third sound, not exactly corresponding with either, as for instance "Julia," which is neither "Juli*ay*" nor "Juli*ah*" exactly. Here are a few:—Angelica, Basilica, sciatica, area, Omega (?), assafœtida, apocrypha, cyclopædia, regalia, paraphernalia, battalia, aurelia, parabola, cupola, nebula, phenomena, ephemera, amphora, plethora, etc.

A1 (as "a," definite article[18]), rhymes AY, EY, EIGH, EH, appliqué and similar French words; but A2 (as in "mamma"), rhymes AH, baa, ha, ah, la, papa, mamma, huzza, psha.

AB, or ABB.

(As in "cab"), bab,§ cab, dab, Mab, gab,§ nab, blab,§ crab, drab,§ scab, stab, shab,§ slab, St Abb. (As in "squab"), see OB.§

ABE.

Babe, astrolabe.

AC.

Rhymes ACK, zodiac, maniac, demoniac, ammoniac, almanac, symposiac, hypochondriac, aphrodisiac, crack, lac.

ACE.

Ace, dace, pace, face, lace, mace, race, brace, chace, grace, place, Thrace, space, trace, apace, deface, efface, disgrace, displace, misplace, embrace, grimace, interlace, retrace, populace, carapace, base, case, abase, debase, etc.

ACH.

(As in "attach"), rhymes ATCH, attach, detach, batch, match, etc. (As in "brach"), rhymes AC, ACK, brach.

ACHE.

(As in "ache"), rhymes EAK, AKE, AQUE. (As in "tache"), rhymes ASH, tache,† patache,† panache.| |

ACK.

Back, brack,† hack, jack, lack, pack, quack, tack, sack, rack, black, clack,§ crack, knack, slack, snack,§ stack, track, wrack, attack, zodiac, demoniac, symposiac, almanac, smack, thwack,§ arrack.

ACS.

Genethliacs, rhymes AX, ACKS, plural of nouns, or third person singular present of verbs in ACK, AC.

ACT.

Act, fact, fract,† pact, tract, attract, abstract, extract, compact, contract, subact, co-act, detract, distract, exact, protract, enact, infract, subtract, transact, retract, charact,§ re-act, cataract, counteract, the preterites and participles of verbs in ACK.

AD, or ADD.

(As in "bad"), add, bad, dad,§ gad, fad,§ had, lad, mad, pad, sad, brad, clad, glad, plaid (?), cad,§ chad,† etc. (As in "wad"), rhymes OD, ODD, quad,¶ wad.

ADE.

Cade, fade, made, jade, lade, wade, blade, bade, glade, shade, spade, trade, degrade, evade, dissuade, invade, persuade, blockade, brigade, estrade, arcade, esplanade, cavalcade, cascade, cockade, crusade, masquerade, renegade, retrograde, serenade, gambade, brocade, ambuscade, cannonade, pallisade, rhodomontade,§ aid, maid, raid, braid, afraid, etc. and the preterites and participles of verbs in AY, EY, and EIGH. [The word "pomade" still retains the French "ade," and rhymes with huzzaed, psha'd, baad.]

ADGE.

Badge, cadge,§ fadge.§

ADZE.

Adze, rhymes plural of nouns, or third person singular present of verbs, in AD, ADD.

AEN.

Ta'en, rhymes AIN, ANE, AIGN, EIGN.

AFE.

Safe, chafe, vouchsafe, waif, nafe,† naif,| | etc.

AFF.

Gaff, chaff, draff, graff, quaff, staff, distaff, engraff, epitaph, cenotaph, paragraph, laugh, half, calf. [Here varieties of pronunciation interfere, some giving the short vowel "chăff," others the long "chāff."]

AFT.

Aft, haft, raft, daft,* waft, craft, shaft, abaft, graft, draft, ingraft, handicraft, draught, and the preterites and participles of verbs in AFF and AUGH, etc.

AG.

Bag, cag, dag,† fag, gag, hag, jag, lag, nag, quag,* rag, sag,† tag, wag, brag, crag, drag, flag, knag, shag, snag, stag, swag,§ scrag,§ Brobdingnag.

AGD.

Smaragd,† preterites and participles of verbs in AG.

AGE.

Age, cage, gage, mage,† page, rage, sage, wage, stage, swage, assuage, engage, disengage, enrage, presage, appanage, concubinage, heritage, hermitage, parentage, personage, parsonage, pasturage, patronage, pilgrimage, villanage, equipage, and gauge.

AGM.

Diaphragm,¶ rhymes AM, AHM.

AGUE.

Plague, vague.

AHM.

Brahm,| | rhymes AM, AGM.

AH.

Ah, bah, pah, rhymes A.

AI.

Serai,|| almai,|| ai,|| papai,|| ay.

AIC

[Really, a dissyllable], haic,|| caic,|| alcaic,¶ saic.|| See AKE.

AID, see ADE and AD. AIGHT, see ATE. AIGN, see ANE.

AIL.

Bail, brail,¶ fail, grail,† hail, jail, mail, nail, pail, quail, rail, sail, shail,† tail, wail, flail, frail, snail, trail, assail, avail, detail, bewail, entail, prevail, aventail,† wassail,† retail, countervail, curtail, Abigail,§ ale, bale, dale, gale, hale, male, pale, sale, tale, vale, wale, scale, shale, stale, swale,† whale, wale,† impale, exhale, regale, veil, nightingale, etc.

AIM, see AME.

AIN.

Cain, blain, brain, chain, fain, gain, grain, lain, main, pain, rain, vain, wain, drain, plain, slain, Spain, stain, swain, train, twain, sprain, strain, abstain, amain, attain, complain, contain, constrain, detain, disdain, distrain, enchain, entertain, explain, maintain, ordain, pertain, obtain, refrain, regain, remain, restrain, retain, sustain, appertain, thane,† Dane, bane, cane, crane, fane, Jane, lane, mane, plane, vane, wane, profane, hurricane, etc., deign, arraign, campaign, feign, reign, vein, rein, skein, thegn,† etc.

AINST.

Against, rhymes abbreviated second person singular present of verbs in AIN, ANE, AIGN, EIN, EIGN

AIQUE.

Caique,|| see AIC.

AINT.

Ain't,§ mayn't,§ faint, plaint, quaint, saint, taint, teint, acquaint, attaint, complaint, constraint, restraint, distraint, feint.

AIR and AIRE, see ARE, EAR, EIR, AIR, ERE, EER.

AIRD.

Laird,* rhymes preterites and participles of verbs in AIR, etc.

AIRN.

Bairn,* cairn.*

AISE, see AZE.

AISLE.

Aisle, see ILE.

AIT, see ATE, EIGHT.

AITH.

Faith, wraith, rath,† baith.*

AIZE, see AZE.

AK.

Dâk,| | rhymes ALK.

AKE.

Ake, bake, cake, hake, lake, make, quake, rake, sake, take, wake, brake, drake, flake, shake, snake, stake, strake,† spake,† awake, betake, forsake, mistake, partake, overtake, undertake, bespake, mandrake, break, steak, etc. See AIC.

AL.

Shall, pal,§ mall (?), sal, gal,§ fal-lal,§ cabal, canal, animal, admiral, cannibal, capital, cardinal, comical, conjugal, corporal, criminal, critical, festival, fineal, funeral, general, hospital, interval, liberal, madrigal, literal, magical, mineral, mystical, musical, natural, original, pastoral, pedestal, personal, physical, poetical, political, principal, prodigal, prophetical, rational, satirical, reciprocal, rhetorical, several, temporal, tragical, tyrannical, carnival, schismatical, whimsical, arsenal, and many others.

ALD.

(As in "bald"), bald, scald, rhymes the preterites and participles of verbs in ALL, AUL, and AWL. (As in "emerald"), rhymes preterite and participle of "cabal," etc.

ALE, see AIL.

ALF.

Calf, half, behalf, staff, laugh, epitaph, etc.

ALK.

Balk, chalk, stalk, talk, walk, calk, dâk,|| baulk, caulk, catafalque, hawk, auk.

ALL.

All, ball, call, gall, caul, haul, appal, enthral, bawl, brawl, crawl, scrawl, sprawl,§ squall.

ALM, ALMS.

Calm, balm, becalm, psalm, palm, embalm, etc.; plurals and third persons singular rhyme with ALMS, as alms, calms, becalms, etc.

ALP.

Scalp, Alp.

ALQUE.

Catafalque, see ALK.

ALSE.

False, valse.

ALT.

(As in "halt"), halt, malt, exalt, salt, vault, assault, default, and fault. (As in "shalt"), asphalt, alt,¶ shalt.

ALVE.

(As in "calve"), calve, halve, salve. (As in "valve"), valve, alve.†

AM.

Am, dam, ham, pam,¶ ram, Sam, cram, dram, flam,§ sham, swam, kam,† clam, epigram, anagram, damn, lamb.

AMB.

Lamb, jamb, oriflamb,† am, dam, etc.

AME.

Blame, came, dame, same, flame, fame, frame, game, lame, name, prame,|| same, tame, shame, inflame, became, defame, misname, misbecame, overcame, aim, claim, maim, acclaim, declaim, disclaim, exclaim, proclaim, reclaim.

AMM.

Lamm,† see AM.

AMME.

Oriflamme,| | see AM.

AMN.

Damn, see AM.

AMP.

(As in "camp"), camp, champ, cramp, damp, stamp, vamp,§ lamp, clamp, decamp, encamp, etc. (As in "swamp"), swamp, pomp, romp.

AN.

(As in "ban"), ban, can, Dan, fan, man, Nan, pan, ran, tan, van, bran, clan, plan, scan, span, than, unman, foreran, began, trepan, courtesan, partisan, artisan, pelican, caravan, shandydan,* barracan¶ (As in "wan"), wan, swan, on, upon, etc.

ANCE.

Chance, dance, glance, lance, trance, prance, intrance, romance, advance, mischance, complaisance, circumstance, countenance, deliverance, consonance, dissonance, extravagance, ignorance, inheritance, maintenance, temperance, intemperance, exorbitance, ordinance, concordance, sufferance, sustenance, utterance, arrogance, vigilance, expanse, enhance, France. [Here the "ance" is pronounced differently by different people, "ănce" and "ānce."]

ANCH.

Branch, staunch, launch, blanch, haunch, paunch,§ ganch.*

AND.

(As in "band"), and, band, hand, land, rand, sand, brand, bland, grand, gland, stand, strand, command, demand, countermand, disband, expand, withstand, understand, reprimand, contraband, and preterites and participles of verbs in AN. (As in "wand"), wand, fond, bond, etc., and the preterites and participles of verbs in ON.

ANE, see AIN.

ANG.

Bang, fang, gang, hang, pang, tang,§ twang, sang, slang,§ rang, harangue, swang, stang,* lang,* chang,| | clang.

ANGE.

Change, grange, range, strange, estrange, arrange, exchange, interchange.

ANGUE.

Harangue, rhyme ANG.

ANK.

Yank,* bank, rank, blank, shank, clank, dank, drank, slank, frank, spank,§ stank, brank,¶ hank, lank, plank, prank, rank, thank, disrank, mountebank, etc.

ANSE, see ANCE.

ANT.

(As in "ant"), ant, cant, chant, grant, pant, plant, rant, slant, aslant, complaisant, displant, enchant, gallant, implant, recant, supplant, transplant, absonant, adamant, arrogant, combatant, consonant, cormorant, protestant, significant, visitant, covenant, dissonant, disputant, elegant, elephant, exorbitant, conversant, extravagant, ignorant, insignificant, inhabitant, militant, predominant, sycophant, vigilant, petulant, etc. (As in "can't"), can't, shan't, aunt, haunt, etc. (As in "want"), want, upon't, font.

AP.

(As in "cap"), cap, dap, gap, hap, lap, map, nap, pap, rap, sap, tap, chap, clap, trap, fap,† flap, knap,§ slap, snap, wrap, scrap, strap, enwrap, entrap, mishap, affrap, mayhap, etc. (As in "swap"), swap, top, chop, etc.

APE.

Ape, cape, shape, grape, rape, scape, scrape, escape, nape, chape,† trape,† jape,§ crape, tape, etc.

APH, see AFF.

APSE.

Apse,¶ lapse, elapse, relapse, perhaps, and the plurals of nouns and third persons singular present tense of verbs in AP.

APT.

Apt, adapt, etc. Rhymes, the preterites and participles of verbs in AP.

AQUE.

Opaque, plaque,¶ make, ache, break.

AR.

(As in "bar"), rhymes Czar,|| bar, car, far, jar, mar, par, tar, spar, scar, star, char, afar, debar, petar,§ unbar, catarrh, particular, perpendicular, secular, angular, regular, popular, singular, titular, vinegar, scimetar, calendar, avatar,|| cinnabar, caviare,|| are. (As in "war"), rhymes for, and perhaps bore, pour, etc.

ARB.

Barb, garb, rhubarb, etc.

ARCE.

Farce, parse, sarse,† sparse. ["Scarce" has no rhyme.]

ARCH.

(As in "march"), arch, march, larch, parch, starch, countermarch, etc. (As in "hierarch"), hierarch, heresiarch, park, ark, etc.

ARD.

(As in "bard"), bard, card, guard, hard, lard, nard, shard, yard, basilard,† bombard, discard, regard, interlard, retard, disregard, etc., and the preterites and participles of verbs in AR. (As in "ward"), ward, sward, afford, restored, etc.

ARE.

(As in "bare"), rhymes care, dare, fare, gare,† hare, mare, pare, tare, ware, flare, glare, scare, share, snare, spare, square, stare, sware, yare,† prepare, aware, beware, compare, declare, ensnare, air, vair,¶ fair, hair, lair, pair, chair, stair, affair, debonnair, despair, impair, glaire, repair, etc.; bear, pear, swear, tear, wear, forbear, forswear, etc.; there, were, where, ere, e'er, ne'er, elsewhere, whate'er, howe'er, howsoe'er, whene'er, where'er, etc,; heir, coheir, their. (As in "are"), rhymes AR.

ARES.

Unawares. Rhymes, theirs, and the plurals of nouns and third persons singular of verbs in are, air, eir, ear.

ARF.

Dwarf, wharf.

ARGE.

Barge, charge, large, marge, targe,† discharge, o'er-charge, surcharge, enlarge.

ARK.

Ark, bark, cark,† clark, dark, lark, mark, park, chark,† shark, spark, stark, embark, remark, etc.

ARL.

Carl,† gnarl, snarl, marl, harl,¶ parle.†

ARM.

(As in "arm"), arm, barm, charm, farm, harm, alarm, disarm. (As in "warm"), warm, swarm, storm, etc.

ARN.

(As in "barn"), barn, yarn, etc. (As in "warn"), warn, forewarn, horn, morn, etc.

ARP.

(As in "carp"), carp, harp, sharp, counterscarp, etc. (As in "warp"), warp, thorp,* etc.

ARRH.

Catarrh, bar, jar.

ARSE, see ARCE.

ARSH.

Harsh, marsh, etc.

ART.

(As in "art"), heart, art, cart, dart, hart, mart, part, smart, tart, start, apart, depart, impart, dispart, counterpart. (As in "wart"), wart, thwart, quart, swart, port, fort, court, short, retort, sport, etc.

ARTH.

Swarth, forth, north.

ARVE.

Carve, starve.

AS.

(As in "was"), was, 'cos,§ poz.§ (As in "gas"), gas, lass, ass, alias. (As in "has"), has, as.

ASE, see ACE.

ASH.

(As in "ash"), ash, cash, dash, clash, crash, flash, gash, gnash, hash, lash, plash, bash,† pash,† brash,† rash, thrash, slash, trash, abash, etc. (As in "wash"), wash, bosh,§ squash,§ quash,¶ swash.†

ASK.

Ask, task, task, cask, flask, mask, hask.†

ASM.

Chasm, spasm, miasm, enthusiasm, cataplasm, phantasm.

ASP.

Asp, clasp, rasp, gasp, grasp, hasp, wasp (?).

ASQUE.

Casque, mask, etc.

ASS.

Ass, brass, class, grass, lass, mass, pass, alas, amass, cuirass, repass, surpass, morass, etc.

AST.

(As in "cast"), cast, last, blast, mast, past, vast, fast, aghast, avast,¶ forecast, overcast, outcast, repast, the preterites and participles of verbs in ASS. (As in "wast"), wast, tost, lost, etc.

ASTE.

Baste, chaste, haste, paste, taste, waste, distaste, waist, and the preterites and participles of verbs in ACE, ASE.

AT.

(As in "at"), at, bat, cat, hat, fat, mat, pat, rat, sat, tat, vat, brat, chat, flat, lat, sprat, that, gnat. (As in "what"), what, spot, not, etc.

ATCH.

(As in "catch"), catch, match, hatch, latch, patch, scratch, smatch, snatch, despatch, ratch,† slatch,¶ swatch, attach, thatch. (As in "watch"), watch, botch,§ Scotch.

ATE.

Bate, date, fate, gate, grate, hate, mate, pate,§ plate, prate, rate, sate, state, scate,† slate, abate, belate, collate, create, debate, elate, dilate, estate, ingrate, innate, rebate,¶ relate, sedate, translate, abdicate, abominate, abrogate, accelerate, accommodate, accumulate, accurate, adequate, affectionate, advocate, adulterate, aggravate, agitate, alienate, animate, annihilate, antedate, anticipate, antiquate, arbitrate, arrogate, articulate, assassinate, calculate, capitulate, captivate, celebrate, circulate, coagulate, commemorate, commiserate, communicate, compassionate, confederate, congratulate, congregate, consecrate, contaminate, corroborate, cultivate, candidate, cooperate, celibate, considerate, consulate, capacitate, debilitate, dedicate, degenerate, delegate, deliberate, denominate, depopulate, dislocate, deprecate, discriminate, derogate, dissipate, delicate, disconsolate, desolate, desperate, educate, effeminate, elevate, emulate, estimate, elaborate, equivocate, eradicate, evaporate, exaggerate, exasperate, expostulate, exterminate, extricate, facilitate, fortunate, generate, gratulate, hesitate, illiterate, illuminate, irritate, imitate, immoderate, impetrate, importunate, imprecate, inanimate, innovate, instigate, intemperate, intimate, intimidate, intoxicate, intricate, invalidate, inveterate, inviolate, legitimate, magistrate, meditate, mitigate, moderate, necessitate, nominate, obstinate, participate, passionate, penetrate, perpetrate, personate, potentate, precipitate, predestinate, predominate, premeditate, prevaricate, procrastinate, profligate, prognosticate, propagate, recriminate, regenerate, regulate, reiterate, reprobate, reverberate, ruminate, separate, sophisticate, stipulate, subjugate, subordinate, suffocate, terminate, titivate,§ tolerate, vindicate, violate, unfortunate, bait, strait, waite, await, great, tête-à-tête, eight,|| weight, straight. [Ate (from "cat") rhymes "yet."]

ATH.

(As in "bath"), bath, path, swath,* wrath. (As in "hath"), hath, aftermath. (As in "rath"), rath, faith, etc.

ATHE.

Bathe, swathe, rathe,† scathe.

AUB.

Daub, kebaub,|| Punjaub.

AUD.

Fraud, laud, applaud, defraud, broad, abroad, and the preterites and participles of verbs in AW, etc.

AUGH.

(As in "laugh"), laugh, quaff, etc. (As in "usquebaugh"), usquebaugh,* law, etc.

AUGHT.

(As in "draught"), draught, quaffed, etc. (As in "caught"), caught, ought, taut, haught,§ etc.

AUK.

Auk, squauk,§ chalk, hawk, etc.

AULM.

Haulm, shawm.

AULK.

Caulk, see ALK.

AULT, see ALT

AUN.

Aun,† shaun,* lawn, prawn, dawn, etc.

AUNCH, see ANCH.

AUND.

Maund,* preterites and participles of verbs in AWN.

AUNCE.

Askaunce, romance, glance, etc.

AUNT.

Aunt, daunt, gaunt, haunt, jaunt, taunt, vaunt, avaunt, shan't, can't, slant, aslant.

AUR.

Bucentaur,|| before, explore, soar.

AUSE.

Cause, pause, clause, applause, because, the plurals of nouns and third persons singular of verbs in AW.

AUST.

Holocaust, frost, cost.

AUZE.

Gauze, cause, laws, etc.

AVE.

Cave, brave, gave, grave, crave, lave, nave, knave, pave, rave, save, shave, slave, stave, wave, behave, deprave, engrave, outbrave, forgave, misgave, architrave. ["Have" is without a rhyme.]

AW.

Craw, daw, law, chaw,§ claw, draw, flaw, gnaw, jaw, maw, paw, raw, saw, scraw,† shaw, straw, thaw, withdraw, foresaw, usquebaugh.*

AWD, see AUD. AWK, see ALK.

AWL.

Bawl, brawl, drawl, crawl, scrawl, sprawl, squaul,§ ball, call, fall, gall, small, hall, pall, tall, wall, stall, install, forestall, thrall, inthrall.

AWM.

Shawm, see AULM.

AWN.

Dawn, brawn, fawn, pawn, spawn, drawn, yawn, awn, withdrawn.

AX.

Ax, tax, lax, pax,¶ wax, relax, flax, the plurals of nouns and third persons singular of verbs in ACK.

AY.

Bray, clay, day, dray, tray, flay, fray, gay, hay, jay, lay, may, nay, pay, play, ray, say, way, pray, spray, slay, stay, stray, sway, tway,† fay,† affray, allay, array, astray, away, belay,¶ bewray, betray, decay, defray, delay, disarray, display, dismay, essay, forelay, gainsay, inlay, relay, repay, roundelay, Twankay,|| virelay, neigh, weigh, inveigh, etc.; prey, they, convey, obey, purvey, survey, disobey, grey, aye, denay.†

AZE.

Craze, draze, blaze, gaze, glaze, raze, maze, amaze, graze, raise, praise, dispraise, phrase, paraphrase, etc., and the nouns plural and third persons singular of the present tense of verbs in AY, EIGH, and EY.

E.

E, see EE.

CRE. CHRE, TRE.

Sepulchre, massacre, theatre, stir, err, fur, myrrh, etc.

EA.

(As in "sea"), sea, see, free, etc. (As in "yea"), yea, way, obey, neigh, etc.

EACE, see EASE.

EACH.

Beach, breach, bleach, each, peach, preach, teach, impeach, beech, leech, speech, beseech.

EAD.

(As in "bread"), bread, shed, wed, dead, etc. (As in "read"), read, secede, feed, etc.

EAF.

(As in "sheaf"), rhymes IEF. (As in "deaf"), rhymes EF.

EAGUE.

League, Teague, etc., intrigue, fatigue, renege,§ etc.

EAK.

(As in "beak"), beak, speak, bleak, creak, freak, leak, peak, sneak,§ squeak, streak, weak, tweak,§ wreak, bespeak, cheek, leek, eke,† creek, meek, reek, seek, sleek, pique,|| week, shriek. (As in "break"), break, take, sake, etc.

EAL.

Deal, heal, reveal, meal, peal, seal, steal, teal, veal, weal, squeal,§ leal,* zeal, repeal, conceal, congeal, repeal, anneal, appeal, wheal,* eel, heel, feel, keel, kneel, peel, reel, steal, wheel. [Real is a dissyllable, and therefore does not count here.]

EALD.

Weald,* see IELD.

EALM.

Realm, elm, whelm.

EALTH.

Health, wealth, stealth, commonwealth, etc.

EAM.

Bream, cream, gleam, seam, scream, stream, team, beam, dream, enseam,† scheme, theme, blaspheme, extreme, supreme, deem, teem, beseem, misdeem, esteem, disesteem, redeem, seem, beteem,† etc.

EAMT.

Dreamt, exempt, attempt, empt,† etc.

EAN.

Bean, clean, dean, glean, lean, mean, wean, yean, demean, unclean, convene, demesne, intervene, mien, hyen,† machine, keen, screen, seen, skean,† green, spleen, between, careen, teen,† foreseen, serene, obscene, terrene, queen, spleen, etc.

EANS.

Means, rhymes plural of nouns, and third persons singular present of verbs, in EAN, EEN, ENE.

EANSE.

Cleanse, plural of nouns, and third person singular present of verbs, in EN.

EANT, see ENT. EAP, see EEP. EAR see EER and AIR.

EARCH.

Search, perch, research, church, smirch,† etc.

EARD.

(As in "heard"), heard, herd, sherd,† etc., the preterites and participles of verbs in ER, UR, etc. (As in "beard"), beard, feared, revered, weird, preterites and participles of verbs in EAR, ERE, etc.

EARL.

Earl, pearl, girl, curl,† churl, whirl, purl,§ furl, etc.

EARN, see ERN. EARSE, see ERSE. EART, see ART.

EARTH.

Earth, dearth, birth, mirth, worth, Perth, berth, etc.

EASE (sounded EACE. For hard "s," see EEZE).

Cease, lease, release, grease, decease, decrease, increase, release, surcease, peace, piece, niece, fleece, geese, frontispiece, apiece, etc.

EAST.

East, feast, least, beast, priest, the preterites and participles of verbs in EASE (sounded EACE).

EAT.

(As in "bleat"), bleat, eat, feat, heat, meat, neat, seat, treat, wheat, beat, cheat, defeat, estreat, escheat, entreat, retreat, obsolete, replete, concrete, complete, feet, fleet, greet, meet, sheet, sleet, street, sweet, discreet. (As in "great"), great, hate, bate, wait, tête.| |

EATH.

(As in "breath"), breath, death, saith, Elizabeth, etc., and antiquated third person singular present, accented on the antepenult, *e.g.*, "encountereth." (As in "heath"), heath, sheath, teeth, wreath, beneath.

EATHE.

Breathe, sheathe, wreathe, inwreathe, bequeathe, seethe, etc.

EAU.

Beau,|| bureau,|| though, go, show, doe, etc.

EAVE.

Cleave, heave, interweave, leave, weave, bereave, inweave, receive, conceive, deceive, perceive, eve, grieve, sleeve, thieve, aggrieve, achieve, believe, disbelieve, relieve, reprieve, retrieve.

EB, and EBB.

Web, neb,* ebb, bleb,† etc.

ECK, and EC.

Beck, peck, neck, check, fleck, deck, speck, wreck, hypothec,|| spec,§ geck.§

EKS.

I'fecks,§ third person singular of verbs and plural of nouns in ECK.

ECT.

Sect, affect, correct, incorrect, collect, deject, detect, direct, disrespect, disaffect, dissect, effect, elect, eject, erect, expect, indirect, infect, inspect, neglect, object, project, protect, recollect, reflect, reject, respect, select, subject, suspect, architect, circumspect, direct, intellect, the preterites and participles of verbs in ECK, etc.

ED.

Bed, bled, fed, fled, bred, Ted, red, shred, shed, sped, wed, abed, inbred, misled, said, bread, dread, dead, head, lead, read, spread, thread, tread, behead, o'erspread, and the preterites and participles of verbs, which, when the "éd" (pronounced) is added, have the accent on the antepenultimate [*e.g.*, vanishéd; but see Chap. VIII.]

EDE.

Glede, rede,† brede,† discede, see EED, EAD.

EDGE.

Edge, wedge, fledge, hedge, ledge, pledge, sedge, allege, kedge,¶ privilege, sacrilege, sortilege, etc.

EE.

Bee, free, glee, knee, see, three, thee, tree, agree, decree, degree, disagree, flee, foresee, o'ersee, pedigree, he, me, we, she, be, jubilee, lee, ne,† sea, plea, flea, tea, key, cap-à-pie,‖ gree,† dree,† calipee.

EECE, see EASE. EECH, see EACH.

EED.

Creed, deed, indeed, bleed, breed, feed, heed, meed, need, reed, speed, seed, steed, weed, proceed, succeed, exceed, knead, read, intercede, precede, recede, concede, impede, supersede, bead, lead, mead, plead, etc.

EEF, see IEF. EEK, see EAK. EEL, see EAL.

EEM, see EAM. EEN, see EAN.

EEP.

Creep, deep, sleep, keep, peep, sheep, steep, sweep, weep, asleep, cheap, heap, neap,¶ etc.

EER.

(As in "beer"), beer, deer, fleer,† geer, jeer, peer, mere, leer, sheer, steer, sneer, cheer, veer, pickeer, domineer, cannoneer, compeer, engineer, mutineer, pioneer, privateer, charioteer, chanticleer, career, mountaineer, fere,† here, sphere, adhere, cohere, interfere, persevere, revere, austere, severe, sincere, hemisphere, &c.; ear, clear, dear, fear, here, near, sear, smear, spear, tear, rear, year, appear, besmear, bandolier,† disappear, endear, auctioneer. (As in "e'er"), ne'er, ARE, AIR, etc.

EESE, see EEZE. EET, see EAT. EETH, see

EATH. EETHE, see EATHE. EEVE, see EAVE.

EEVES.

Eeaves, rhymes plural of nouns, and third person singular present of verbs in EEVE, IEVE, etc.

EEZE.

Breeze, freeze, wheeze, sneeze, squeeze, and the plurals of nouns and third persons singular present tense of verbs in EE, cheese, leese,† these, ease, appease, disease, displease, tease, seize, etc., and the plurals of nouns in EA, EE, etc.

EF.

Clef,¶ nef,† semibref,¶ kef,‖ deaf, etc.

EFT.

Cleft, left, theft, weft, bereft, etc.

EG, and EGG.

Egg, leg, beg, peg, Meg, keg.

EGE.

Renege,§ see EAGUE.

EGM.

Phlegm, apothegm, parapegm, diadem, etc.

EGN.

Thegn,|| vain, mane, etc.

EH.

Eh? rhymes A, AY, EY, EIGH.

EIGH, see AY. EIGHT, see ATE and ITE. EIGN,
see AIN. EIL, see EEL and AIL. EIN, see
AIN. EINT, see AINT. EIR, see ARE.

EIRD.

Weird, see EARD.

EIT, see EAT. EIVE, see EAVE. EIZE,
see EEZE. EKE, see EAK.

EL, and ELL.

Ell, dwell, fell, hell, knell, quell, sell, bell, cell, mell,† dispel, foretell, excel,
compel, befell, yell, well, tell, swell, spell, smell, shell, parallel, sentinel,
infidel, citadel, refel, repel, rebel, impel, expel, asphodel, petronel,† calomel,
muscatel.

ELD.

Held, geld, withheld, upheld, beheld, eld,§ etc., the preterites and
participles of verbs in EL, ELL.

ELF.

Elf, delf, pelf,§ self, shelf, himself, etc.

ELK.

Elk, kelk,† whelk, etc.

ELM.

Elm, helm, realm, whelm, overwhelm, etc.

ELP.

Help, whelp, kelp,* yelp, etc.

ELT.

Belt, gelt,| | melt, felt, welt,¶ smelt, pelt, dwelt, dealt.

ELVE.

Delve, helve, shelve, twelve, etc.

ELVES.

Elves, themselves, etc., the plurals of nouns and third persons singular of verbs in ELVE.

EM.

Gem, hem, stem, them, diadem, stratagem, anadem, kemb,† phlegm, condemn, contemn, etc.

EME, see EAM.

EMN.

Condemn, contemn, gem, hem, them. See EM, etc.

EMPT.

Tempt, exempt, attempt, contempt, dreamt.

EN.

Den, hen, fen, ken, men, pen, ten, then, when, wren, denizen. [Hyen§ rhymes EEN.]

ENCE.

Fence, hence, pence, thence, whence, defence, expense, offence, pretence, commence, abstinence, circumference, conference, confidence, consequence, continence, benevolence, concupiscence, difference, diffidence, diligence, eloquence, eminence, evidence, excellence, impenitence, impertinence, impotence, impudence, improvidence, incontinence, indifference, indigence, indolence, inference, intelligence, innocence, magnificence, munificence, negligence, omnipotence, penitence, preference, providence, recompense, reference, residence, reverence, vehemence, violence, sense, dense, cense, condense, immense, intense, propense, dispense, suspense, prepense, incense, frankincense.

ENCH.

Bench, drench, retrench, quench, clench, stench, tench, trench, wench, wrench, intrench, blench.†

END.

Bend, mend, blend, end, fend,† lend, rend, send, spend, tend, vend, amend, attend, ascend, commend, contend, defend, depend, descend, distend, expend, extend, forefend, impend, mis-spend, obtend, offend, portend, pretend, protend, suspend, transcend, unbend, apprehend, comprehend, condescend, discommend, recommend, reprehend, dividend, reverend, friend, befriend, and the preterites and participles of verbs in EN, etc.

ENDS.

Amends, the plurals of nouns and third persons singular present tense of verbs in END.

ENE, see EAN.

ENGE.

Avenge, revenge, no rhyme.

ENGTH.

Length, strength, etc.

ENS.

Lens, plural of nouns, and third person singular present of verbs, in EN.

ENT

Bent, lent, rent, pent, scent, sent, shent,† spent, tent, vent, went, blent, cement, brent,† hent,† absent, meant, ascent, assent, attent, augment, cement, content, consent, descent, dissent, event, extent, foment, frequent, indent, intent, invent, lament, mis-spent, o'erspent, present, prevent, relent, repent, resent, ostent, ferment, outwent, underwent, discontent, unbent, circumvent, represent, abstinent, accident, accomplishment, admonishment, acknowledgment, aliment, arbitrement, argument, banishment, battlement, blandishment, astonishment, armipotent, bellipotent, benevolent, chastisement, competent, complement, compliment, confident, continent, corpulent, detriment, different, diligent, disparagement, document, element, eloquent, eminent, equivalent, establishment, evident, excellent, excrement, exigent, experiment, firmament, fraudulent, government, embellishment, imminent, impenitent, impertinent, implement, impotent, imprisonment, improvident, impudent, incident, incompetent, incontinent, indifferent, indigent, innocent, insolent, instrument, irreverent, languishment, ligament, lineament, magnificent, management, medicament, malecontent, monument, negligent, nourishment, nutriment, occident, omnipotent, opulent, ornament, parliament, penitent, permanent, pertinent, president, precedent, prevalent, provident, punishment, ravishment, regiment, resident, redolent, rudiment, sacrament, sediment, sentiment, settlement, subsequent, supplement, intelligent, tenement, temperament, testament, tournament, turbulent, vehement, violent, virulent, reverent.

ENTS.

Accoutrements, the plurals of nouns and third persons singular present tense of verbs in ENT.

EP.

Step, nep, skep,* rep, demirep,§ etc.

EPE.

Clepe,† keep, reap, etc.

EPT.

Accept, adept, except, intercept, crept, sept,* slept, wept, kept, etc.

ER, and ERR.

Her, sir, fir, burr, cur, err, aver, defer, infer, deter, inter, refer, transfer, confer, prefer, whirr, administer, waggoner, islander, arbiter, character, villager, cottager, dowager, forager, pillager, voyager, massacre, gardener, slanderer, flatterer, idolater, provender, theatre, amphitheatre, foreigner, lavender, messenger, passenger, sorcerer, interpreter, officer, mariner, harbinger, minister, register, canister, chorister, sophister, presbyter, lawgiver, philosopher, artrologer, loiterer, prisoner, grasshopper, astronomer, sepulchre, thunderer, traveller, murderer, usurer.

ERCH, see EARCH. ERCE, see ERSE. IERCE,

see ERSE. ERD, see EARD. ERE, see EER.

ERF.

Serf, turf, surf, scurf, etc.

ERGE.

Verge, absterge,† emerge, immerge, dirge, urge, purge, surge.

ERGUE.

Exergue,† burgh.

ERM.

Term, firm, worm, etc.

ERN.

Fern, stern, discern, hern,† concern, learn, earn, yearn, quern,* dern,† burn, turn, etc.

ERNE.

Eterne,† see ERN.

ERP.

Discerp,† see IRP.

ERSE.

Verse, absterse, adverse, averse, converse, disperse, immerse, perverse, reverse, asperse, intersperse, universe, amerce, coerce, hearse, purse, curse, etc.

ERT.

Wert, advert, assert, avert, concert, convert, controvert, desert, divert, exert, expert, insert, invert, pervert, subvert, shirt, dirt, hurt, spurt,§ etc.

ERTH.

Berth, birth, mirth, earth, worth, etc.

ERVE.

Serve, nerve, swerve, preserve, deserve, conserve, observe, reserve, disserve, subserve, curve, etc.

ES, ESS, or ESSE.

Yes, bless, dress, cess,* chess, guess, less, mess, press, stress, acquiesce, access, address, assess, compress, confess, caress, depress, digress, dispossess, distress, excess, express, impress, oppress, possess, profess, recess, repress, redress, success, transgress, adultress, bashfulness, bitterness, cheerfulness, comfortless, comeliness, dizziness, diocess, drowsiness, eagerness, easiness, ambassadress, emptiness, evenness, fatherless, filthiness, foolishness, forgetfulness, forwardness, frowardness, fruitfulness, fulsomeness, giddiness, greediness, gentleness, governess, happiness, haughtiness, heaviness, idleness, heinousness, hoariness, hollowness, holiness, lasciviousness, lawfulness, laziness, littleness, liveliness, loftiness, lioness, lowliness, manliness, masterless, mightiness, motherless, motionless, nakedness, neediness, noisomeness, numberless, patroness, peevishness, perfidiousness, pitiless, poetess, prophetess, ransomless, readiness, righteousness, shepherdess, sorceress, sordidness, spiritless, sprightliness, stubbornness, sturdiness, surliness, steadiness, tenderness, thoughtfulness, ugliness, uneasiness, unhappiness, votaress, usefulness, wakefulness, wantonness, weaponless, wariness, willingness, wilfulness, weariness, wickedness, wilderness, wretchedness, drunkenness, childishness, duresse,| | cesse.†

ESE, see EEZE.

ESH.

Flesh, fresh, refresh, thresh, afresh, nesh,† mesh.

ESK, and ESQUE.

Desk, grotesque, burlesque, arabesque, picturesque, moresque, etc.

EST.

Best, chest, crest, guest, jest, nest, pest, quest, rest, test, vest, lest, west, arrest, attest, bequest, contest, detest, digest, divest, invest, palimpsest,¶ alcahest,| | infest, molest, obtest, protest, request, suggest, unrest, interest, manifest, breast, abreast, etc., and the preterites and participles of verbs in ESS.

ET.

Bet, get, jet, fret, let, met, net, set, wet, whet, yet, debt, abet, beget, beset, forget, regret, alphabet, amulet, anchoret, cabinet, epithet, parapet, rivulet, violet, coronet, parroquet, basinet, wagonette,| | cadet, epaulette, piquette, sweat, threat, etc.

ETCH.

Fetch, stretch, wretch, sketch, etc.

ETE.

Effete, see EAT.

ETH.

Elizabeth, see EATH.

ETTE.

Rosette, silhouette,| | wagonette,| | cassolette,| | bet, etc.

EVE, see EAVE.

EUCE.

Deuce, see USE.

EUD.

Feud, rude, mood, stewed, etc.

EUM.

Rheum, see OOM, UME.

EUR.

Amateur,| | connoisseur,| | bon-viveur.| |

EW.

Blew, chew, dew, brew, drew, flew, few, grew, new, knew, hew, Jew, mew,† view, threw, yew, crew, slew, anew, askew, bedew, eschew, renew, review, withdrew, screw, interview, emmew,† clue, due, cue, glue, hue, rue, sue, true, accrue, ensue, endue, imbue, imbrue, pursue, subdue, adieu, purlieu,| | perdue,| | residue, avenue, revenue, retinue, through, pooh, you. [News takes plural of nouns, and third person singular present of verbs, of this class.]

EWD.

Flewd,§ lewd, screwed, see UDE.

EWN.

Hewn, see UNE.

EX.

Sex, vex, annex, convex, complex, perplex, circumflex, and the plurals of nouns and third persons singular of verbs in EC, ECK.

EXT.

Next, pretext, and the preterites and participles of verbs in EX.

EY.

(As in "prey"), rhymes AY, A. (As in "key"), rhymes EE, EA.

EYNE.

Eyne,§ rhymes INE.

I.

I.

Alibi,| | alkali,| | try, eye, high, bye, vie, etc.

IB.

Bib, crib, squib, drib,§ glib,§ nib, rib.

IBE.

Bribe, tribe, kibe,† scribe, ascribe, describe, superscribe, prescribe, proscribe, subscribe, transcribe, inscribe, imbibe, diatribe.

IC.

Catholic, splenetic, heretic, arithmetic, brick, etc.

ICE.

Ice, dice, mice, nice, price, rice, spice, slice, thrice, trice, splice, advice, entice, vice, device, concise, precise, paradise, sacrifice, etc.

ICHE and ICH, see ITCH.

ICK.

Brick, sick, chick, kick, lick, nick, pick, quick, stick, thick, trick, arithmetic, choleric, catholic, heretic, rhetoric, splenetic, lunatic, politic.

ICT.

Strict, addict, afflict, convict, inflict, contradict, Pict, etc. The preterites and participles of verbs in ICK, etc.

ID.

Bid, chid, hid, kid, lid, slid, rid, bestrid, pyramid, forbid, quid,§ squid, katydid,|| etc.

IDE.

Bide, chide, hide, gride,† glide, pride, ride, slide, side, nide,† stride, tide, wide, bride, abide, guide, aside, astride, beside, bestride, betide, confide, decide, deride, divide, preside, provide, subside, misguide, subdivide, etc., the preterites and participles of verbs in IE, IGH, and Y.

IDES.

Ides, besides, the plurals of nouns and third persons singular of verbs in IDE, etc.

IDGE.

Bridge, ridge, midge, fidge,§ abridge, etc.

IDST.

Midst, amidst, didst, etc., the second persons singular of the present tense of verbs in ID.

IE, or Y.

By, buy, cry, die, dry, eye, fly, fry, fie, hie, lie, pie, ply, pry, rye, shy, sly, spy, sky, sty, tie, try, vie, why, ally, apply, awry, bely, comply, decry, defy, descry, deny, imply, espy, outvie, outfly, rely, reply, supply, untie, amplify, beautify, certify, crucify, deify, dignify, edify, falsify, fortify, gratify, glorify, indemnify, justify, magnify, modify, mollify, mortify, pacify, petrify, purify, putrify, qualify, ratify, rectify, sanctify, satisfy, scarify, signify, specify, stupefy, terrify, testify, verify, vilify, vitrify, vivify, prophesy, high, nigh, sigh, thigh. [Such words as "lunacy," "polygamy," "tyrrany," cannot well be used, as it is difficult to get the "y" sound without over-accentuating it.]

IECE, see EASE.

IED.

Pied, side, sighed, rhymes with preterites and participles of verbs in Y or IE.

IEF.

Grief, chief, fief,† thief, brief, belief, relief, reef, beef, leaf, sheaf, etc.

IEGE.

Liege, siege, assiege, besiege.

IELD.

Field, yield, shield, wield, afield, weald,* and the preterites and participles of verbs in EAL.

IEN, see EEN.

IEND.

(As in "fiend"), rhymes preterites and participles of verbs in EAN, EEN. (As in "friend"), rhymes END.

IER.

Pier, bier, tier, rhymes EER.

IERCE.

Fierce, pierce, tierce.

IEST.

Priest, rhymes EAST. ("Diest," second person singular present, at times pronounced as a monosyllable, rhymes "spiced," etc.)

IEVE.

(As in "sieve"), rhymes "give," see IVE. (As in "grieve"), rhymes EVE, EAVE.

IEU, IEW.

Lieu,|| review, rhyme EW, UE, etc.

IEZE.

Frieze, rhymes EEZE, etc.

IF, IFF.

If, skiff, stiff, whiff, cliff, sniff,§ tiff,§ hieroglyph.

IFE.

Rife, fife, knife, wife, strife, life.

IFT.

Gift, drift, shift, lift, rift, sift, thrift, adrift, etc., and the preterites and participles of verbs in IFF.

IG.

Big, dig, gig, fig, pig, rig,§ sprig, twig, swig,§ grig,* Whig, wig, jig, prig.

IGE.

Oblige, no rhyme.

IGH, see IE. IGHT, see ITE.

IGM.

Paradigm, rhymes IME.

IGN, see INE. IGUE, see EAGUE.

IKE.

Dike, like, pike, spike, strike, alike, dislike, shrike, glike.†

IL, ILL.

Bill, chill, fill, drill, gill, hill, ill, kill, mill, pill, quill, rill, shrill, fill, skill, spill, still, swill,§ thrill, till, trill, will, distil, fulfil, instil, codicil, daffodil.

ILCH.

Filch, milch.

ILD.

(As in "child"), rhymes mild, wild, etc., the preterites and participles of verbs of one syllable in ILE, or of more syllables, provided the accent be on the last. (As in "gild"), rhymes build, rebuild, etc., and the preterites and participles of verbs in ILL.

ILE.

Bile, chyle,¶ file, guile, isle, mile, pile, smile, stile, style, tile, vile, while, awhile, compile, revile, defile, exile, erewhile, reconcile, beguile, aisle. [There is also the "eel" sound, as in imported words like bastile,|| pastile,|| rhyming with EEL, EAL.]

ILGE.

Bilge, no rhyme.

ILK.

Milk, silk, bilk,§ whilk,* etc.

ILN.

Kiln, no rhyme.

ILT.

Gilt, jilt, built, quilt, guilt, hilt, spilt, stilt, tilt, milt.

ILTH.

Filth, tilth, spilth, etc.

IM.

Brim, dim, grim, him, rim, skim, slim, trim, whim, prim, limb, hymn, limn.

IMB.

(As in "limb"), rhymes IM. (As in "climb"), rhymes IME.

IME.

Chime, time, grime,§ climb, clime, crime, prime, mime, rhyme, slime, thyme, lime, sublime.

IMES.

Betimes, sometimes, etc. Rhymes the plurals of nouns and third persons singular present tense of verbs in IME.

IMN, see IM.

IMP.

Imp, limp, pimp,§ gimp, jimp.

IMPSE.

Glimpse. Rhymes, the plurals of nouns and third persons singular present tense of verbs in IMP.

IN, INN.

Bin, chin, din, fin, gin, grin, in, inn, kin, pin, shin, sin, spin, skin, linn,* thin, twin, tin, win, within, javelin, begin, whin, baldachin,† cannikin.

INC.

Zinc, rhymes INK.

INCE.

Mince, prince, since, quince, rinse, wince, convince, evince.

INCH.

Clinch, finch, winch, pinch, inch.

INCT.

Instinct, distinct, extinct, precinct, succinct, tinct,† &c., and the preterites and participles of certain verbs in INK, as linked, pinked, &c.

IND.

(As in "bind"), find, mind, blind, kind, grind, rind, wind, behind, unkind, remind, etc., and the preterites and participles of verbs in INE, IGN, etc. (As in "rescind"), preterites and participles of verbs in IN.

INE.

Dine, brine, mine, chine, fine, line, nine, pine, shine, shrine, kine, thine, trine, twine, vine, wine, whine, combine, confine, decline, define, incline, enshrine, entwine, opine, recline, refine, repine, superfine, interline, countermine, undermine, supine, concubine, porcupine, divine, sign, assign, consign, design, eyne,† condign, indign.† [There is also the short "inc," as in "discipline," rhyming IN.]

ING.

Bring, sing, cling, fling, king, ring, sling, spring, sting, string, ging,† swing, wing, wring, thing, etc., and the participles of the present tense in ING, with the accent on the antepenultimate, as "recovering."

INGE.

Cringe, fringe, hinge, singe, springe, swinge,§ tinge, twinge, infringe.

INK.

Ink, think, wink, drink, blink, brink, chink, clink, link, pink, shrink, sink, slink, stink, bethink, forethink, skink,† swink.†

INQUE.

Cinque, appropinque, see INK.

INSE.

Rinse, see INCE.

INT.

Dint, mint, hint, flint, lint, print, squint, asquint, imprint, sprint,¶ quint.¶

INTH.

Plinth,¶ hyacinth, labyrinth.||

INX.

Minx,§ sphinx,|| jinks,§ plural of nouns, and third person singular present of verb in INK.

IP.

Chip, lip, hip, clip, dip, drip, lip, nip, sip, rip, scrip, ship, skip, slip, snip, strip, tip, trip, whip, equip, eldership, fellowship, workmanship, rivalship, and all words in SHIP with the accent on the antepenultimate.

IPE.

Gripe, pipe, ripe, snipe, type, stripe, wipe, archetype, prototype.

IPSE.

Eclipse. Rhymes, the plurals of nouns and third persons singular present tense in IP.

IQUE.

Oblique, clique,|| critique,|| bézique,|| antique, pique,|| see EAK.

IR, see UR. IRCH, see URCH. IRD, see URD.

IRE.

Fire, dire, hire, ire, lyre, mire, quire, sire, spire, squire, wire, tire, attire, acquire, admire, aspire, conspire, desire, inquire, entire, expire, inspire, require, retire, transpire, pyre, gipsire,† gire.†

IRGE, see ERGE.

IRK.

Dirk, firk,§ kirk, stirk,* quirk,§ shirk, work, burke, murk.

IRL.

Girl, whirl,* twirl, curl, furl, churl, thirl,* etc.

IRM.

Firm, affirm, confirm, infirm, worm, term, chirm,† etc.

IRP.

Chirp, see URP.

IRR.

Whirr, skirr,§ see UR.

IRST, See URST. IRT, see URT.

IRTH.

Birth, mirth, earth, dearth, worth.

IS, pronounced like IZ.

Is, his, whiz.

ISS.

Bliss, miss, hiss, kiss, this, abyss, amiss, submiss, dismiss, remiss, wis,† Dis, spiss.†

ISC.

Disc, whisk, risk, see ISK.

ISE, see ICE and IZE.

ISH.

Dish, fish, wish, cuish,† pish,§ squish.§

ISK.

Brisk, frisk, disc, risk, whisk, basilisk, tamarisk.

ISM.

Chrism, solecism, anachronism, abysm, schism, syllogism, witticism, criticism, organism, heroism, prism, egotism, cataclysm.

ISP.

Crisp, wisp, lisp.

IST.

Fist, list, mist, twist, wrist, assist, consist, desist, exist, insist, persist, resist, subsist, alchemist, amethyst, anatomist, antagonist, annalist, evangelist, eucharist, exorcist, herbalist, humorist, oculist, organist, satirist, etc., and the preterites and participles of verbs in ISS, etc.

IT.

Bit, Cit,§ hit, fit, grit, flit, knit, pit, quit, sit, split, twit, wit, chit,§ whit, writ, admit, acquit, commit, emit, omit, outwit, permit, remit, submit, transmit, refit, benefit, perquisite.

ITCH.

Ditch, pitch, rich, which, flitch, itch, stitch, switch, twitch, witch, bewitch, niche, enrich, fitch.

ITE, and IGHT.

Bite, cite, kite, blite, mite, quite, rite, smite, spite, trite, white, write, contrite, disunite, despite, indite, excite, incite, invite, polite, requite, recite, unite, reunite, aconite, appetite, parasite, proselyte, expedite, blight, benight, bright, fight, flight, fright, height, light, knight, night, might, wight, plight, right, tight, slight, sight, spright, wight, affright, alight, aright, foresight, delight, despite, unsight, upright, benight, bedight,† oversight, height, accite,§ pight.§

ITH.

Pith, smith, frith,* sith.† ("With" has strictly no rhyme.)

ITHE.

Hithe, blithe, tithe, scythe, writhe, lithe.

ITS.

Quits, rhymes plural of nouns, and third person singular, present of verbs in IT.

IVE.

(As in "five"), rhymes dive, alive, gyve, hive, drive, rive, shrive, strive, thrive, arrive, connive, contrive, deprive, derive, revive, survive. (As in "give"), rhymes live, sieve, fugitive, positive, sensitive, etc.

IX.

Fix, six, mix, nix,§ affix, infix, prefix, transfix, intermix, crucifix, etc., and the plurals of nouns and third persons singular of verbs in ICK.

IXT.

Betwixt. Rhymes, the preterites and participles of verbs in IX.

ISE, and IZE.

Prize, wise, rise, size, guise, disguise, advise, authorise, canonise, agonise,§ chastise, civilise, comprise, criticise, despise, devise, enterprise, excise, exercise, idolise, immortalise, premise, revise, signalise, solemnise, surprise, surmise, suffice, sacrifice, sympathise, tyrannise, and the plurals of nouns and third persons singular present tense of verbs in IE or Y.

O

Mo',† calico, bo,§ portico, go, ago, undergo, ho, though, woe, adagio,¶ seraglio,|| owe, beau, crow, lo, no, fro',† so.

OACH.

Broach, coach, poach, abroach, approach, encroach, reproach, loach.

OAD, see ODE.

OAF.

Oaf,† loaf.

OAK.

Cloak, oak, croak, soak, joke, see OKE.

OAL, see OLE. OAM, see OME. OAN, see ONE.

OAP, see OPE. OAR, see ORE. OARD, see

ORD. OAST, see OST. OAT, see OTE.

OATH.

Oath, loath, both, see OTH.

OAVES.

Loaves, groves, roves, cloves, etc.

OAX.

Hoax, coax, rhymes plural of nouns, and third person singular present of verbs in OKE.

OB.

Cob, fob,§ bob, lob, hob, nob, mob, knob, sob, rob, throb, cabob,|| swab,¶ squab.§

OBE.

Globe, lobe, probe, robe, conglobe.

OCE, see OSE.

OCH.

Loch,* epoch, see OCK.

OCHE.

Caroche,|| gauche.||

OCK.

Block, lock, cock, clock, crock, dock, frock, flock, knock, mock, rock, shock, stock, sock, brock, hough.

OCT.

Concoct, rhymes the preterites and participles of verbs in OCK.

OD.

Cod, clod, God, rod, sod, trod, nod, plod, odd, shod, quod,§ pod, wad, quad,§ odd, hod, tod.*

ODE.

Bode, ode, code, mode, rode, abode, corrode, explode, forebode, commode, incommode, episode, à-la-mode,|| road, toad, goad, load, etc., and the preterites and participles of verbs in OW, OWE.

ODGE.

Dodge,§ lodge, Hodge, podge,§ bodge.†

OE.

(As in "shoe"), rhymes OO. (As in "toe"), rhymes foe, doe, roe, sloe, mistletoe, OWE and OW.

OFF.

Doff, off, scoff, cough, etc.

OFT.

Oft, croft, soft, aloft, etc., and the preterites and participles of verbs in OFF, etc.

OG.

Hog, bog, cog,† dog, clog, fog, frog, log, jog,§ agog,§ Gog, prog,§ quog,* shog,§ tog,§ pollywog,* dialogue, epilogue, synagogue, catalogue, pedagogue.

OGE.

Gamboge, rouge.

OGUE.

(As in "rogue"), rhymes vogue, prorogue, collogue,* disembogue. (As in "catalogue"), rhymes OG.

OH.

Oh, rhymes OW and OWE.

OICE.

Choice, voice, rejoice.

OID.

Void, avoid, devoid, asteroid, alkaloid, etc., and the preterites and participles of verbs in OY.

OIF.

Coif,¶ no rhyme.

OIGN.

Coign,|| rhymes OIN.

OIL.

Oil, boil, coil, moil, soil, spoil, toil, despoil, embroil recoil, turmoil, disembroil.

OIN.

Coin, join, subjoin, groin, loin, adjoin, conjoin, disjoin, enjoin, foin,† proin,† purloin, rejoin.

OINT.

Oint, joint, point, disjoint, anoint, appoint, aroint,† disappoint, counterpoint.¶

OIR.

(As in "choir"), rhymes IRE, but the foreign sound, as in "devoir," "reservoir," is nearer AR, but must not be so rhymed. "Coir" is a dissyllable.

OISE.

Poise, noise, counterpoise, equipoise, etc., and the plurals of nouns and third persons singular present tense of verbs in OY. ["Turquoise" would rhyme with plurals of AH, etc.]

OIST.

Hoist, moist, foist,§ the preterites and participles of verbs in OICE.

OIT.

Doit,§ exploit, adroit, quoit, etc.

OKE.

Broke, choke, smoke, spoke, stroke, yoke, bespoke, invoke, provoke, revoke, cloak, oak, soak.

OL.

Alcohol, loll,§ doll, extol, capitol, Moll, Poll, etc.

OLD.

Old, bold, cold, gold, hold, mold, scold, sold, told, behold, enfold, unfold, uphold, withhold, foretold, manifold, marigold, preterites and participles of verbs in OLL, OWL, OLE, and OAL.

OLE.

Bole, dole, jole, hole, mole, pole, sole, stole, whole, shoal, cajole, girandole,|| condole, parole,|| patrole,|| pistole,|| console,|| aureole,|| vole,* coal, foal, goal, bowl, roll, scroll, toll, troll, droll, poll, control, enrol, soul, etc.

OLL.

(As in "loll"), rhymes OL. (As in "droll"), rhymes OLE.

OLN.

Stol'n, swoln.

OLP.

Holp,† golpe.¶

OLT.

Bolt, colt, jolt, holt, dolt,§ revolt, thunderbolt, moult.

OLVE.

Solve, absolve, resolve, convolve, involve, devolve, dissolve, revolve.

OM.

OM is by general consent degraded to UM; Tom, from, Christendom, aplomb.|| But for "whom," see OOM.

OMB.

(As in "tomb"), see OOM. (As in "comb"), see OME, clomb. (As in "bomb"), see UM. "Rhomb" has no rhyme. (As in "aplomb"| |), see OM.

OME.

Dome, home, mome, foam, roam, loam.

OMP.

Pomp, swamp, romp.

OMPT.

Prompt, preterite and participle of romp.

ON.

(As in "don"), rhymes on, con, upon, anon, bonne;| | (as in "won"), rhymes ton, fun, done, etc. [By some, "gone," "hone," and other like words are so pronounced as to rhyme with "on."]

ONCE.

(As in "sconce"), rhymes response, etc. (As in "once"), rhymes dunce, etc.

ONCH.

Conch, jonque.¶

OND.

Pond, bond, fond, beyond, abscond, correspond, despond, diamond, vagabond, etc., and the preterites and participles of verbs in ON.

ONDE.

Blonde,| | rhymes OND.

ONE.

Prone, bone, drone, throne, alone, stone, tone, lone, zone, atone, enthrone, dethrone, postpone, grown, flown, disown, thrown, sown, own, loan, shown, overthrown, groan, blown, moan, known, cone, loan, etc. [With regard to "gone" and "shone," some pronounce them so that they rhyme with "one" others so that the first rhymes with "lawn," and the second with "prone."]

ONG.

(As in "long"), rhymes prong, song, thong, strong, throng, wrong, along, belong, prolong. (As in "among"), rhymes hung, tongue, etc.

ONGE.

Sponge, see UNGE.

ONGUE, see UNG.

ONK.

(As in "monk"), rhymes "drunk." (As in "conk"§), rhymes jonque.¶

ONQUE.

Jonque,¶ see ONK.

ONSE.

Response, sconce, ensconce.

ONT.

(As in "font"), rhymes want. (As n "front"), rhymes punt, etc. [The abbreviated negatives, won't, don't, rhyme together.]

OO.

Coo, woo, shoe, two, too, who, do, ado, undo, through, you, true, blue, flew, stew, etc. See O, UE, EW, etc.

OOCH, see OACH.

OOD.

(As in "brood"), rhymes mood, food, rood, feud, illude, etc., the preterites and participles of verbs in OO, and EW, UE, etc. (As in "wood"), rhymes good, hood, stood, withstood, understood, could, would, brotherhood, livelihood, likelihood, neighbourhood, widowhood. (As in "blood"), rhymes flood, cud, mud, etc.

OOF.

Hoof, proof, roof, woof, aloof, disproof, reproof, behoof.

OOH.

Pooh,§ rhymes EW, etc.

OOK.

Book, brook, cook, crook, hook, look, rook, shook, took, mistook, undertook, forsook, stook,* betook.

OOL.

Cool, fool, pool, school, stool, tool, befool, spool,† buhl,|| pule, rule.

OOM.

Gloom, groom, loom, room, spoom,† bloom, doom, tomb, entomb, whom, womb, plume, spume, etc.

OON, see UNE.

Boon, soon, moon, noon, spoon, swoon, buffoon, lampoon, poltroon, tune, prune, coon,§ June, hewn, dune,* shalloon, dragoon.

OOP.

Loop, poop, scoop, stoop, troop, droop, whoop, coop, hoop, soup, group, dupe.

OOR.

(As in "boor"), rhymes poor, moor, tour,|| amour, paramour,|| contour, pure, sure, your, etc. (As in "door"), rhymes floor, bore, pour, etc.

OOSE.

Goose, loose, juice, truce, deuce, noose, use, profuse, seduce, etc.

OOT.

(As in "root"), rhymes boot, coot, hoot, loot,|| shoot, toot,§ suit, fruit, lute, impute, etc. (As in "foot"), rhymes put. [It is difficult to say whether "soot" should rhyme "root" or "but," the pronunciation so varies.]

OOTH.

(As in "booth"), rhymes smooth, soothe, etc. (As in "tooth"), rhymes youth, uncouth, truth.

OOVE.

Groove, see OVE.

OOZE.

Ooze, noose, whose, choose, lose, use, abuse, the plurals of nouns and third persons singular present tense of verbs in EW, UE.

OP.

Chop, hop, drop, crop, fop,§ top, pop, prop, flop,§ shop, slop sop, stop, swop,§ underprop.

OPE.

Hope, cope, mope, grope, pope, rope, scope, slope, trope, aslope, elope, interlope, telescope, heliotrope, horoscope, antelope, etc., and ope, contracted in poetry for open.

OPH.

Soph,¶ see OFF.

OPT.

Adopt, rhymes with the preterites and participles of verbs in OP, etc.

OQUE.

Equivoque, see OAK.

OR.

Or, for, creditor, counsellor, competitor, emperor, ancestor, ambassador, progenitor, conspirator, conqueror, governor, abhor, metaphor, bachelor, senator, etc., and every word in OR having the accent on the last, or last syllable but two, pour, bore, tore, boar, hoar, war, corps,│ │ tor.*

ORB.

Orb, sorb,¶ corb.†

ORCE, see ORSE.

ORCH.

Scorch, torch, porch, etc.

ORD.

(As in "cord"), rhymes lord, record, accord, abhorr'd, hoard, board, aboard, ford, afford, sword, and the preterites and participles of verbs in OAR, ORE. (As in "word"), rhymes bird, stirred, absurd, erred, curd, etc.

ORDE.

Horde, see ORD.

ORE.

Bore, core, gore, lore, more, ore, pore, score, shore, snore, sore, store, swore, tore, wore, adore, afore, ashore, deplore, explore, implore, restore, forebore, foreswore, heretofore, hellebore, sycamore, albicore, boar, oar, roar, soar, four, door, floor, o'er, orator, senator, abhor.

ORGE.

George, gorge, disgorge, regorge, forge.

ORK.

Ork,† cork, fork, stork, pork.

ORLD.

World, rhymes with the preterites and participles of verbs in URL and IRL.

ORM.

(As in "form"), rhymes storm, conform, deform, inform, perform, reform, misinform, uniform, multiform, transform. (As in "worm"), rhymes "term," ERM.

ORN.

Born, corn, morn, horn, scorn, thorn, adorn, suborn, unicorn, sorn,¶ capricorn, shorn, torn, worn, lorn, forlorn, lovelorn, sworn, foresworn, overborne, foreborne, mourn.

ORP.

Thorp,* rhymes ARP.

ORPS.

Corps,|| rhymes ORE.

ORPSE.

Corpse, rhymes plurals of nouns, and preterites and participles of verbs in ARP.

ORSE.

Horse, endorse, unhorse, force, remorse, coarse, course, torse,† morse,† corse, etc.

ORST, see URST.

ORT.

Short, sort, exhort, consort, distort, extort, resort retort, snort, mort,|| wart, fort, port, court, report.

ORTS.

Orts,† plural of nouns, and third person singular present of verbs in ORT.

ORTH.

(As in "north"), rhymes fourth. (As in "worth"), rhymes birth, earth, &c.

OSE.

(As in "jocose"), rhymes close, dose, morose, gross, engross, verbose. (As in "pose"), rhymes close, dose, hose, chose, glose, froze, nose, prose, those, rose, compose, depose, disclose, dispose, discompose, expose, impose, enclose, interpose, oppose, propose, recompose, repose, suppose, transpose, arose, presuppose, foreclose, etc., and the plurals of nouns and apostrophised preterites and participles of verbs in OW, OE, O, etc. (As in "lose"), rhymes use, etc. See OOZE, USE.

OSH.

Bosh,§ wash, &c.

OSM.

Microcosm,|| no rhyme.

OSQUE, OSK.

Mosque,|| kiosk.||

OSS.

Boss, cross, dross, moss, loss, across, albatross, doss,§ emboss.

OST.

(As in "cost"), rhymes frost, lost, accost, etc., and the preterites and participles of words in OSS. (As in "ghost"), rhymes post, most, coast, and second person singular present of verbs in OW, as ow'st. (As in "dost"), rhymes UST.

OT.

Clot, cot, blot, got, hot, jot, lot, knot, not, plot, pot, scot, shot, polyglot, sot,§ spot, apricot, trot, rot, grot, begot, forgot, allot, complot, yacht, quat,§ melilot, counterplot.

OTCH.

Botch,§ notch, crotch,† blotch, Scotch, watch.

OTE.

Note, vote, lote,† mote, quote, rote, wrote, smote, denote, tote,* promote, remote, devote, anecdote, antidote, boat, coat, bloat, doat, float, gloat, goat, oat, overfloat, afloat, throat, moat.

OTH.

(As in "broth"), rhymes cloth, froth, troth, wrath. (As in "both"), rhymes loth, sloth, oath, growth. ["Moth" has no rhyme, though at times pronounced to rhyme "cloth."]

OTHE.

Clothe, loathe (with "s" added rhymes "oaths;" though "clothes," the noun, in comic verse may rhyme with "snows," being colloquially spoken "clo's").

OU.

(As in "thou"), see OW. (As in "you"), see OO.

OUBT.

Doubt, see OUT.

OUC.

Caoutchouc, rhymes book.||

OUCH.

Couch, pouch, vouch, slouch,§ avouch, crouch.

OUCHE.

Cartouche,|| buche.¶

OUD.

Shroud, cloud, loud, proud, aloud, crowd, o'er-shroud, etc., and the preterites and participles of verbs in OW.

OUGH has various pronunciations; see OFF, OW,

OWE, OCK, O, EW, and UFF.

OUGE.

(As in "rouge"), rhymes gamboge.

OUGHT.

Bought, thought, ought, brought, forethought, fought, nought, sought, wrought, besought, bethought, methought, aught, naught, caught, taught, &c.

OUL.

(As in "foul"), see OWL. (As in "soul"), see OLE.

OULD.

Mould, fold, old, cold, etc., and the preterites and participles of verbs in OWL, OLL, and OLE.

OULT.

Moult. See OLT.

OUN.

Noun, see OWN.

OUNCE.

Bounce,§ flounce, renounce, pounce, ounce, denounce, pronounce.

OUND.

(As in "bound"), rhymes found, mound, ground, hound, pound, round, sound, wound (verb), abound, aground, around, confound, compound, expound, profound, rebound, resound, propound, surround, etc., and the preterites and participles of verbs in OWN. (As in "wound"—the noun), rhymes preterites and participles of verbs in OON, UNE. etc.

OUNG.

Young, see UNG.

OUNT.

Count, mount, fount, amount, dismount, remount, surmount, account, discount, miscount, account.

OUP.

Stoup,† group, see OOP.

OUPH, or OUPHE.

Ouphe or ouph,† see OOF.

OUQUE.

Chibouque,|| see UKE.

OUR.

(As in "hour"), rhymes lour, sour, our, scour, deflow'r, devour, bow'r, tow'r, etc. (As in "pour"), rhymes bore, more, roar, pour, war, etc. (As in "tour"), rhymes your, amour,|| contour, pure, etc.

OURGE.

Scourge, rhymes URGE.

OURN.

(As in "adjourn"), rhymes URN. (As in "mourn"), rhymes ORN.

OURNE.

Bourne,† rhymes ORN.

OURS.

(As in "ours"), rhymes the plurals of nouns and third persons singular present tense of verbs in OUR and OW'R. (As in "yours"), rhymes the plurals of nouns and third persons singular present tense of verbs in URE, OOR, etc.

OURSE.

Course, see ORSE.

OURT.

Court, see ORT.

OURTH.

Fourth, see ORTH.

OUS.

Nous,§ house, mouse, chouse,§ douse,§ etc.

OUSE.

(As in "house"—noun), rhymes nous.§ (As in "spouse"), rhymes browze, and plural of nouns and third persons singular present of verbs in OW.

OUST.

Joust,† rhymes UST.

OUT.

Bout, stout, out, clout, pout, gout, grout, rout, scout, shout, tout,§ snout,§ spout, stout, sprout, trout, about, devout, without, throughout, doubt, redoubt, misdoubt, drought, &c.

OUTH.

(As in "mouth"—noun), rhymes south, drouth, etc. (As in "youth"), rhymes truth. (As in "mouth"—verb), no rhyme.

OVE.

(As in "wove"), rhymes inwove, interwove, hove, alcove, clove, grove, behove, rove, stove, strove, throve, drove. (As in "dove"), rhymes love, shove, glove, above. (As in "move"), rhymes approve, disprove, disapprove, improve, groove, prove, reprove, etc.

OW.

(As in "now"), rhymes bow, how, mow, cow, brow, sow, vow, prow, avow, allow, trow, disallow, endow, bough, plough, slough (mire), thou, etc. (As in "blow"), rhymes stow, crow, bow, flow, glow, grow, know, low, mow, row, show, sow, strow, slow, snow, throw, below, bestow, foreknow, outgrow, overgrow, overflow, overthrow, reflow, foreshow, go, no, toe, foe, owe, wo, oh, so, lo, though, hoe, ho, ago, forego, undergo, dough, roe, sloe, and sew.

OWD.

Crowd, see OUD.

OWE.

Owe, see OW.

OWL.

(As in "cowl"), rhymes growl, owl, fowl, howl, prowl, scowl, fowl, &c. (As in "bowl"), rhymes soul, hole, goal, dole.

OWN.

(As in "brown"), rhymes town, clown, crown, down, drown, frown, gown, adown, renown, embrown, noun. (As in "thrown"), rhymes shown, blown, tone, bone, moan, own, etc.

OWSE.

Bowse,¶ rouse, see OUSE.

OWTH.

Growth, oath, both.

OWZE

Blowze, browse, rouse, spouse, carouse, touse,§ espouse, the verbs to house, mouse, etc., and the plurals of nouns and third persons singular present tense of verbs in OW.

OX.

Ox, box, fox, equinox, orthodox, heterodox, the plurals of nouns and third persons singular present tense of verbs in OCK.

OY.

Boy, buoy,¶ coy, employ, cloy, joy, toy, alloy, annoy, convoy, decoy, destroy, enjoy, employ.

OYNT.

Aroynt,† see OINT.

OYLE.

Scroyle,† see OIL.

OYNE.

Royne,† see OIN.

OZ.

(As in "poz"), rhymes was. (As in "coz"), rhymes buzz.

OZE.

Gloze, see OSE.

U.

Ormolu, | | few, adieu, | | lieu, | | through, do, true, too.

UB.

Cub, club, dub, chub, drub,§ grub, hub,§ rub, snub,§ shrub, tub.

UBE.

Cube, tube.

UCE.

Truce, sluice, spruce, deuce, conduce, deduce, induce, introduce, puce, produce, seduce, traduce, juice, reduce, use, abuse, profuse, abstruse, disuse, excuse, misuse, obtuse, recluse.

UCH.

Much, touch, such, see UTCH.

UCK.

Buck, luck, pluck, suck, struck, tuck, truck, duck.

UCT.

Conduct, deduct, instruct, obstruct, aqueduct. The preterites and participles of verbs in UCK.

UD.

Bud, scud, stud, mud, cud, blood, flood. ["Suds" rhymes plurals of nouns and third person present singular of verbs in UD.]

UDE.

Rude, crude, prude, allude, conclude, delude, elude, exclude, exude, snood,† include, intrude, obtrude, seclude, altitude, fortitude, gratitude, interlude, latitude, longitude, magnitude, multitude, solicitude, solitude, vicissitude, aptitude, habitude, ingratitude, inaptitude, lassitude, plenitude, promptitude, servitude, similitude, lewd, feud, brood, etc., and the preterities and participles of verbs in EW, UE, etc.

UDGE.

Judge, drudge, grudge, trudge, adjudge, prejudge, fudge,§ smudge, nudge, budge,§ sludge.*

UE.

True, hue, see EW, OO, etc.

UFF.

Buff, cuff, chuff,§ bluff, huff, gruff, luff,¶ puff, snuff, stuff, ruff, rebuff, counterbuff, rough, tough, enough, slough (cast skin), chough, etc.

UFT.

Tuft, rhymes the preterites and participles of verbs in UFF.

UG.

Lug,§ bug, dug, drug, hug, jug, rug, slug, smug,§ snug, mug, shrug, pug.

UGH.

Pugh (old form of "pooh"), see OO.

UGUE.

Fugue,¶ no rhyme.

UHL.

Buhl,|| see ULE, OOL.

UICE.

Sluice, see USE.

UIDE.

Guide, see IDE.

UILD.

Guild, see ILD.

UILT.

Guilt, see ILT.

UINT.

Squint, see INT.

UISE.

(As in "guise"), see ISE. (As in "bruise"), see USE.

UISH.

Cuish,† see ISH.

UIT.

Fruit, bruit,† suit, see OOT, UTE.

UKE.

Duke, puke,† rebuke, fluke,§ chibouque,|| etc.

UL, and ULL.

(As in "cull"), rhymes dull, gull, hull, lull, mull, null, trull,† skull, annul, disannul. (As in "full"), rhymes wool, bull, pull, bountiful, fanciful, sorrowful, dutiful, merciful, wonderful, worshipful, and every word ending in ful, having the accent on the ante-penultimate.

ULCH.

Mulch,¶ gulch.†

ULE.

Mule, pule,† Yule, rule, overrule, ridicule, misrule, fool, tool, buhl.|| [Gules, heraldic term, rhymes plural of nouns, and third person singular present of verbs in ULE, etc.]

ULF.

Gulf, no rhyme.

ULGE.

Bulge, indulge, divulge, etc.

ULK.

Bulk, hulk, skulk, sulk.

ULM.

Culm,¶ no rhyme.

ULP.

Gulp, sculp, pulp, ensculp.§

ULSE.

Pulse, repulse, impulse, expulse, convulse, insulse.†

ULT.

Result, adult, exult, consult, indult, occult, insult, difficult, catapult,|| etc.

UM.

Crum,† chum,§ drum, glum,§ gum, hum, mum,§ scum, plum, sum, swum, thrum,¶ thumb, dumb, succumb come, become, overcome, burdensome, cumbersome, frolicsome, humoursome, quarrelsome, troublesome, encomium, opium, etc.

UMB.

Dumb, thumb, crumb. See UM.

UME.

Fume, plume, assume, consume, perfume, resume, presume, deplume, room, doom, tomb, rheum.

UMP.

Bump, pump, jump, lump, plump, rump, stump, trump, thump, clump.

UN.

Dun, gun, nun, pun, run, sun, shun, tun, stun, spun, begun, son, won, ton, done, one, none, undone.

UNCE.

Dunce, once, etc.

UNCH.

Bunch, punch, hunch, lunch, munch, scrunch,§ crunch.§

UNCT.

Defunct, disjunct, rhymes preterites and participles of verbs in UNK.

UND.

Fund, refund, preterites of verbs in UN, etc.

UNE.

June, tune, untune, jejune, prune, croon, hewn, swoon, moon, soon, etc.

UNG.

Bung, clung, dung, flung, hung, rung, strung, sung, sprung, slung, stung, swung, wrung, unsung, young, tongue, among.

UNGE.

Plunge, sponge, expunge, etc.

UNK.

Drunk, bunk,§ hunk,§ sunk, shrunk, stunk, punk,† trunk, slunk, funk,§ chunk,* monk. [Hunks,§ rhymes plural of nouns and third person singular present of verbs in UNK.

UNT.

Brunt, blunt, hunt, runt, grunt, front, etc., and (?) wont (to be accustomed).

UOR.

Fluor,¶ rhymes four, bore, roar.

UP.

Cup, sup, pup, dup,† up.

UPT.

Abrupt, corrupt, interrupt, the participles and preterites of verbs in UP, etc.

UR.

Blur, cur, bur, fur, slur, spur, concur, demur, incur, her, whirr, err, sir, stir, fir, sepulchre, etc.

URB.

Curb, disturb, verb, herb, etc.

URCH.

Church, lurch, birch, perch, search, smirch.§

URD.

Curd, absurd, bird, gird,§ word, and the preterites and participles of verbs in UR and IR.

URE.

Cure, pure, dure, lure, sure, abjure, allure, assure, demure, conjure, endure, manure, inure, insure, immature, immure, mature, obscure, procure, secure, adjure, calenture, coverture, epicure, investiture, forfeiture, furniture, miniature, nourriture, overture, portraiture, primogeniture, temperature, poor, moor, etc.

URF.

Turf, scurf, serf, surf, etc.

URGE.

Purge, urge, surge, scourge, thaumaturge, gurge,† verge, diverge, etc.

URK.

Lurk, Turk, work, irk,† jerk, perk, quirk, mirk.

URL.

Churl, curl, furl, hurl, purl,§ uncurl, unfurl, earl, girl, twirl, pearl, etc.

URM.

Turm,|| see ERM.

URN.

Burn, churn, spurn, turn, urn, return, overturn, tern, discern, earn, sojourn, adjourn, rejourn.

URP.

Usurp, chirp, extirp, discerp, etc.

URR.

Purr, see UR.

URSE.

Nurse, curse, purse, accurse, disburse, imburse, reimburse, worse, verse, hearse, disperse, etc.

URST.

Burst, curst, durst, accurst, thirst, worst, first, versed, etc.

URT.

Blurt,§ hurt, spurt,§ dirt, shirt, flirt, squirt, wort,¶ vert,¶ etc.

US, or USS.

Pus,¶ us, thus, buss,§ truss, discuss, incubus, overplus, arquebus,† cuss,§ amorous, boisterous, clamorous, credulous, dangerous, ungenerous, generous, emulous, abulous, frivolous, hazardous, idolatrous, infamous, miraculous, mischievous, mountainous, mutinous, necessitous, numerous, ominous, perilous, poisonous, populous, prosperous, ridiculous, riotous, ruinous, scandalous, scrupulous, sedulous, traitorous, treacherous, tyrannous, venomous, vigorous, villanous, adventurous, adulterous, ambiguous, blasphemous, dolorous, fortuitous, gluttonous, gratuitous, incredulous, lecherous, libidinous, magnanimous, obstreperous, odoriferous, ponderous, ravenous, rigorous, slanderous, solicitous, timorous, valorous, unanimous, calamitous.

USE

(As in the noun "use") rhymes disuse, abuse, deuce, truce, sluice, juice, loose, goose, noose, moose. (As in "muse") rhymes the verb use, abuse, loose, choose, shoes, amuse, diffuse, excuse, infuse, misuse, peruse, refuse, suffuse, transfuse, accuse, bruise, and the plurals of nouns and third persons singular of verbs in EW and UE, etc.

USH

(As in "blush") rhymes brush, crush, gush, flush, rush, lush,† tush, frush,† hush. (As in "bush") rhymes push, etc.

USK.

Busk,†; tusk, dusk, husk, musk.

USP.

Cusp,† no rhyme.

UST.

Bust, crust, dust, just, must, lust, rust, thrust, trust, adjust, disgust, distrust, intrust, mistrust, robust, unjust, the preterites and participles of verbs in US, USS, etc.

UT, or UTT.

But, butt, cut, hut, gut, glut, jut, nut, shut, strut, englut, rut, scut,†; slut, smut, abut, and soot.(?)

UTCH.

Hutch, crutch, Dutch, much, such, touch, etc.

UTE.

Brute, lute, flute, mute, acute, compute, confute, dispute, dilute, depute, impute, minute, pollute, refute, salute, absolute, attribute, contribute, constitute, destitute, dissolute, execute, institute, persecute, prosecute, resolute, substitute, fruit, bruit,† suit, recruit, boot, etc., soot(?).

UTH.

Azimuth,¶ rhymes doth.

UX.

Dux,|| crux,|| lux,|| flux, reflux. The plurals of nouns and third persons singular of verbs in UCK.

Y.

Fly, affy,† aby,† see IE, IGH, etc.

YB.

Syb, see IB.

YM.

Sym,† see IM.

YMN.

Hymn, see IM.

YMPH.

Nymph, lymph, etc.

YN.

Baudekyn,† see IN.

YNE.

Anodyne, see INE.

YNX.

Lynx, rhymes plurals of nouns and third persons present singular of verbs in INK.

YP.

Gyp,§ hyp,§ see IP.

YPE.

Type, see IPE.

YPH.

Hieroglyph,|| see IFF.

YPSE.

Apocalypse,|| see IPSE.

YRE.

Lyre, pyre, byre,* see IRE.

YRRH.

Myrrh, her, err, sir, cur, etc.

YSM.

Abysm, cataclysm, schism, etc.

YST.

Amethyst, analyst, cyst, see IST.

YVE.

Gyve, see IVE.

YX.

Sardonyx, pyx, fix, rhymes plural of nouns and third persons singular present of verbs in ICK.

YZE.

Analyze, see ISE.

APPENDIX[19]

ENGLISH VERSIFICATION.

In normal English Verse, the most determinate characteristic is uniformity of syllabic structure. RHYME, indeed, is a common but not an essential adjunct, some of our noblest poems being composed in unrhymed or Blank Verse. MEASURE, RHYTHM, ACCENT, and PAUSE, are all features of much moment in English Versification, but they cannot be reduced to absolutely uniform rules. The variations to which they are subject are many and important. Of the positive and correct signification of the terms Rhyme, Measure, Rhythm, Accent, and Pause, it is needful to give some explanation.

RHYME consists in a likeness or uniformity of sound in the closing, syllable, or syllables, of successive or contiguous lines of verse. We find used, in English poetry, three several sorts of Rhymes, namely, Single, Double, and Treble. Of the first, or one-syllabled rhyme, the following is an example:—

"O, mortals, blind in fate, who never know

To bear high fortune, or endure the low!"

The closing word, however, is not necessarily a monosyllable. There may be two syllables, as here:—

"What though his mighty soul his grief contains,

He meditates revenge who least complains."

Or three:—

"Seeking amid those untaught foresters,

If I could find one form resembling hers."

Or four:—

"We might be otherwise—we might be all

We dream of, happy, high, majestical."

Or there might be any number in this kind of verse under ten, if the long and short (accented and unaccented) syllables were rightly placed, and if the penultimate syllable, in particular, was short or unaccented. It is only to be observed further, that it is the sound in which uniformity is required, and not the spelling. Thus the following words make good rhymes:—made, plaid, and stayed; course, force, and hoarse; ride, lied, dyed; be, glee, lea; lo, blow, foe; beer, clear, here, and so forth. The most perfect single rhymes in our language, however, are those in which the rhyming vowels of two lines, and their closing letter or letters (if there be any), are exactly the same. "So" and "no," "day" and "say," "content" and "unbent," "oculist" and "humorist," "ambassadress" and "unhappiness"—all of these are perfect rhymes, seeing that the consonant preceding the rhyming vowel varies in each pair of words, all being alike after it. This is the criterion of an absolutely perfect rhyme.[20] However, such rhymes as "away" and "sway," "strain" and "drain," "tress" and "dress," are not unfrequently used in good poetry. But those rhymes are held decidedly bad which merely repeat the same sounds, whether the words spell alike or not. Thus "amid" and "pyramid," "light" and "satellite," "maid" and "made," are defective rhymes. In short, it may be laid down as a rule, that, where the immediate consonants are not varied before the vowels in two rhyming lines, the letters before these consonants must be markedly different, as in "strain" and "drain," to make the rhymes at all good. "Away" and "sway," or "loud" and "cloud," though tolerated, are imperfect in a strict sense. No rhymes are more uncertain, it may be observed, than those of words ending in *y*, as "privacy," "remedy," and the like. In monosyllables and dissyllables so ending, as "try" and "rely," the termination always rhymes to *ie*, as in "vie" or "hie;" and it seems right that *y* should always so be rhymed.[21] Nevertheless, it as often rhymes to an *e*, as in "be" and "she." The plural of nouns in *y*, again, having their termination in "ies," rhyme very uncertainly. They are sometimes placed to correspond with "lies," and sometimes with "lees." There is no fixed rule on this subject.

On many other points, also, the student of English poetry must gather information for himself from reading and observation. Of Double Rhymes it is not necessary to say much here. They are formed by adding a short or unaccented syllable to the measure of ordinary verses of any kind, and composing the rhyme out of it and the preceding syllable, now the penultimate one. Thus—

"Then all for women, painting, rhyming, *drinking*,

Besides ten thousand freaks that died in *thinking*."

In grave poetry, which uses the double rhyme occasionally, but on the whole sparingly, the last or short syllable should be entirely alike in double rhymes, and to the penultimate or accented one the same rules should apply as in the case of perfect single rhymes. That is to say, the consonants preceding the accented vowels should be varied, though licenses are taken in this respect. "Trading" and "degrading," for example, would be held a passable rhyme. The unison of sound,[22] and not the spelling, largely guides the formation of double rhymes, even in serious verse. "Liquor" and "thicker," "ever" and "river," "motion" and "ocean," "debtor" and "better," are instances in proof; and many, many worse cases pass muster occasionally. Faulty double rhymes are rendered faulty much in the same way as single ones. Thus, "minion" and "dominion," "million" and "vermilion," are bad rhymes. In burlesque and satiric poetry, a great deal of freedom is used in the composition of double rhymes.[23] Butler often frames them most amusingly in his "Hudibras." For example—

"When pulpit, drum ecclesi*astic,*

Was beat with fists, instead of *a stick.*"

"Though stored with deletery *med'cines,*

Which whosoever took is *dead since.*"

Occasionally in the highest serious verse we find the double rhyme composed of two several words, as in the following specimen from Wordsworth:[24]—

"Through many a long blue field of ether,

Leaving ten thousand stars beneath her."

In light or burlesque pieces, however, as Butler shows, the double rhyme is compounded in any way which gives the sound required. The Treble Rhyme is only found in such pieces. Butler says:—

"There was an ancient sage philosopher,

Who had read Alexander Ross over."

But, as the treble rhyme occurs but three or four times even in "Hudibras," it need not be dilated on here.

The word MEASURE, when employed in reference to poetry, indicates the length of line and general syllabic structure of peculiar kinds and forms of verse. Thus, a piece written in lines of eight syllables is said to be in the octo-syllabic measure, and one of ten-syllabled lines in the deca-syllabic measure. The term RHYTHM, again, denotes the arrangement of the syllables in relation to one another, as far as accentuation is concerned, and the particular cadence resulting from that arrangement. All the common measures of verse have a prevailing and normal rhythm—that is, long and short, or accented and unaccented, syllables follow each other in a certain order of succession. Thus, the normal octo-syllabic measure consists of short and long alternately, as does also the deca-syllabic. But variations, as will be shown, occur in these respects. What rhythm, again, is to measures of verse in the aggregate, ACCENT nearly is to each line specifically and individually. In one and all has the accent its peculiar seat; and the more that seat is varied, generally speaking, the more beautiful is the verse. The PAUSE is another feature of some importance in English poetry. In every line a point occurs, at which a stop or rest is naturally made, and this independently of commas or periods. It will be found impossible to read poetry without making this pause, even involuntarily. The seat of it varies with the accent, seeing that it always follows immediately after the accent From the want of a right distribution of accent and pause verse becomes necessarily and unpleasingly monotonous.

On the whole, English poetry, as remarked, has not one well-marked and unvariable characteristic of structure, saving that syllabic uniformity which distinguishes it in all its accurate forms and phases. However, this feature of our verse has been far from stamping it with anything like sameness. Though our bards have habitually measured their verses by the syllabic scale—with the exception of our old ballad writers, and a few moderns, who have written professedly after their exemplars—yet no language in the world contains stores of poetry more varied than the English in respect of construction. Lines of all lengths, containing from three syllables to twenty, have been tried by our poets, and, in general, pleasingly and successfully. Fletcher has even attempted tri-syllabic verses, though, as may be supposed, only in a slight choral form.

"Move your feet

To our sound,

Whiles we greet

All this ground."

In verses of four syllables, again, pretty long poems have actually been composed, and particularly by John Skelton, a poet of the time of Henry VIII. Much of what he wrote was sheer doggerel, no doubt being rendered so partly by the nature of his own talent and disposition, and partly because his chosen form of verse would scarcely admit of the conveyance of serious sentiments. Now and then, however, he does contrive to make his miniature lines interesting, as in the following address to Mistress Margaret Hussey:—

"Merry Margaret,

As midsummer flower,

Gentle as falcon,

Or hawk of the tower;

With solace and gladness,

Much mirth and no madness.

All good and no badness;

So joyously,

So maidenly,

So womanly,

Her demeaning,

In every thing

Far, far passing

That I can indite

Or suffice to write

Of merry Margaret,

As midsummer flower,

Gentle as falcon,

Or hawk of the tower."

It will be observed that Skelton, while taking four syllables for the basial structure of his lines, uses five occasionally, forming either a dissyllabic ending, or giving two short syllables for a long one, as in the lines—

"Gentle as *falcon*,

Or hawk *of the* tower."

At the same time it will be noticed, that the same number of accents, or accented syllables, is kept up throughout. This will be found to be the case with most of our irregular or ballad compositions. They vary as to the number of syllables, but not of long ones or accents. Scott's romantic poetry exemplifies the same fact, which is a striking one, and explains why the melody of ballad-verses is so little affected by their syllabic irregularities. This law of composition should be specially noted by young cultivators of the Muses. Dryden has used four syllables in verses of the choral order. Thus he says—

"To rule by love,

To shed no blood,

May be extoll'd above;

But here below,

Let princes know,

'Tis fatal to be good."

It is obvious that the four-syllabled line is much too curt to allow of its being habitually used in serious compositions. The same thing may be said of lines of five syllables. They have been, and can only be, introduced in minor pieces. And here it may be observed, that the measure of four syllables, when used gravely, is of simple rhythm, consisting of a short and long syllable alternately, as in the verses of Dryden. Skelton, indeed, has confined himself to no rule. The measure of five syllables necessarily changes its rhythm; and the second and fourth lines of the subjoined stanza show what may be called the normal form of the measure:—

"My love was false, but I was firm

From my hour of birth;

Upon my buried body, lie

Lightly, gentle earth."

Long and short syllables (three long or accented) occur here in alternation, and compose the line in its regular rhythmical shape. Some other lines of an odd number of syllables, as seven, are for the most part similarly framed. But, in these respects, variations are often adopted. For instance, the following five-syllabled verses are differently constructed:—

"Now, now the mirth comes,

With cake full of plums,

Where bean's the king of the sport here;

Besides, we must know,

The pëa also[25]

Must revel as queen in the court here.

"Begin then to choose

This night, as ye use,

Who shall for the present delight here;

Be king by the lot,

And who shall not

Be Twelfth-day queen for the night here."

The first, second, fourth, and fifth lines here do not present alternate long and short syllables, as in the former quotation. But, however poets may indulge in such variations, the alternation of longs and shorts constitutes the proper rhythmical arrangement in the measure of verse now under notice. Without three accents, indeed, the five-syllabled verse becomes but a variety of the four-syllabled, as in Skelton's pieces.

In the measure of six syllables, we find many beautiful pieces wholly and continuously composed, grave as well as gay. Drayton, for example, has a fine "Ode written in the Peaks," of which the ensuing stanza may give a specimen:—

"This while we are abroad,

Shall we not touch our lyre?

Shall we not sing an ode?

Shall all that holy fire,

In us that strongly glow'd

In this cold air expire?"

In a mixed and lyrical shape, the six-syllabled line is also used finely by Shakspeare:—

"Blow, blow, thou winter wind,

Thou art not so unkind

As man's ingratitude;

Thy tooth is not so keen,

Because thou art not seen,

Although thy breath be rude.

Heigh ho! sing heigh ho!"

It is only as we come to consider verses of some length, that the subject of Accent and Pause can be clearly illustrated by examples. The Accent practically consists in either an elevation or a falling of the voice, on a certain word or syllable of a word, when verse is read; and that word or syllable is called the seat of the Accent. The term Rhythm has nothing to do with the sense; whereas the Accent rests mainly on the sense; and on the sense, moreover, of each individual line. The Pause, again, was before stated to be a rest or stop, made in pronouncing lines of verse, and dividing each, as it were, into two parts or hemistiches. Though, in the six-syllabled measure, the brevity of the lines confines the reader in a great degree to the ordinary rhythm, which consists of a short and long syllable alternately, or three unaccented and three accented, yet, in Drayton's ode, though the lines cannot well exemplify the Pause, there is a slight variation in the seat of the Accent—

"Shall we not touch our lyre?

Shall we not sing an ode?"

The accent here plainly falls on the initial "shall," giving force to the interrogation. Shakspeare's "Under the green-wood tree" is similarly accented.

The seven-syllabled measure is one in which many exquisite poems have been composed by English writers. Raleigh used it, as did likewise Shakspeare many incidental passages in his plays, and afterwards Cowley, Waller, and other bards of note. But it was by Milton that the seven-syllabled verse was developed, perhaps, to the greatest perfection, in his immortal "L'Allegro" and "Il Penseroso." In its systematic shape, this species of verse consists of a long and short syllable in alternation, the long beginning and closing each line, and therefore giving four accents. The measure is graceful and easy exceedingly, though apt to become monotonous in enunciation. To obviate this effect, Milton, who, either from natural fineness of ear, or from observation and experience, had acquired a consummate mastery of rhythm, roughened his lines purposely, sometimes by introducing eight syllables, and sometimes by varying the seat of the accent. This will partly be seen in the following brief extracts, which will also show how admirably he could make the measure the vehicle either of the gay or the grave:—

"Haste thee, nymph, and bring with thee

Jest and youthful Jollity,

Quips, and cranks, and wanton wiles,

Nods, and becks, and wreathed smiles,

Such as hang on Hebe's cheek,

And love to live in dimple sleek;

Sport that wrinkled care derides,

And Laughter holding both his sides."

So speaks the poet to Euphrosyne; and now he addresses "divinest Melancholy:"—

"Come, pensive nun, devout and pure,

Sober, steadfast, and demure,

All in a robe of darkest grain,

Flowing with majestic train,

And sable stole of cypress lawn,

Over thy decent shoulders drawn.

Come, but keep thy wonted state,

With even step and musing gait,

And looks commercing with the skies."

It will be observed how finely the dancing effect of the seven-syllabled verse is brought out, in accordance with the sense, in the first quoted passage, and with what skill it is repressed in the second, principally by the use of the graver octosyllabic line. John Keats employed the measure now under consideration very beautifully in his "Ode to Fancy," and gave it variety chiefly by changing the ordinary rhythm. Thus—

"Sit thou by the ingle, when

The sear faggot blazes bright,

Spirit of a winter's night."

The second line, from the position of "sear faggot," is rendered so far harsh, and tends to prevent the "linked sweetness" from being too long drawn out, and cloying the ear. Shakspeare—what under the sun escaped his eye?—had noticed the sing-song proclivities of the seven-syllabled measure, since he makes Touchstone say, on hearing a sample, "I'll rhyme you so eight years together; dinners, and suppers, and sleeping hours excepted; it is the right butter-woman's rank (trot) to market. For a taste." And he gives a taste:—

"If a hart do lack a hind,

Let him seek out Rosalind,

If the cat will after kind,

So, be sure, will Rosalind.

Sweetest nut hath sourest rind,

Such a nut is Rosalind."

"This is the very false gallop of verses," continueth the sententious man of motley. He is partly in the right; but the reader has now been told in what way the great poets, who have employed this measure of verse effectively, overcame the difficulties attending its perfect composition. In speaking of long syllables, they were before called accents; but the reader must guard against confounding these with the proper single accent, occurring in each line, and connected with the sense, as well as with the pause. As exemplifying both such accent and pause in the seven-syllabled line, the following couplets may be cited from Cowley. The accent is on the third syllable, the pause at third and fourth, as marked:—

"Fill the bowl—with rosy wine,

Round our temples—roses twine;

Crown'd with roses—we contemn

Gyges' wealthy—diadem."

These pauses must not be deemed arbitrary. The tongue is compelled to make them in the act of utterance.

The octosyllabic measure has been long the most common, if not the most popular, of all forms of English verse. It was in use among the Romancers of the Middle Ages, before England possessed a national literature, or even a proper national language. "Maister Wace" composed in this measure his "Roman de Rou;" and it was adopted by many of the early

"Rhyming Chroniclers," and "Metrical Romancers" of Great Britain. Father Chaucer also, though his noblest efforts were made in what became the heroic verse (the decasyllabic) of his country, produced many pieces in the eight-syllabled measure; and Gower used it solely and wholly. So likewise did Barbour in his famous history of the Bruce, and Wyntoun in his Metrical Chronicle of Scotland. Since their days to the present, it has been ever a favourite form of verse among us, and, indeed, has been at no period more popular than during the current century. At the same time, poems of the very highest class, epic or didactic, have never been composed in the octosyllabic measure. It wants weight and dignity to serve as a fitting vehicle for the loftiest poetic inspirations. It has been the basis, however, of much of the finest lyrical poetry of England. It has likewise been splendidly wielded for the purposes of satire, as witness the burlesque or comic epos of Butler, and the works of Swift. And, in our own immediate age, it has been magnificently employed by Scott, Moore, Byron, Campbell, and others, in the composition of poetical romances.

Byron spoke of the octosyllabic verse as having about it "a fatal facility"—meaning that, from its simple brevity of construction, it was too apt to degenerate into doggerel. It is almost needless to give examples of a species of poetry so well known. Though the lines thereof are too short to permit of very full variety of cadence or emphasis, yet these are always marked and traceable, more or less. As graceful and flowing octosyllables, the following lines from the "Tam o' Shanter" of Burns have not many equals in our poetry:—

"But pleasures are like poppies spread;

You seize the flower—its bloom is shed;

Or like the snow-falls in the river,

A moment white, then gone for ever;

Or like the Borealis race,

That flit ere you can point their place;

Or like the rainbow's lovely form,

Evanishing amid the storm."

Long and short syllables alternately form the regular rhythm of this kind of verse; but occasional changes of rhythm and accentuation are used by all good writers. In the following lines Andrew Marvel introduces finely such a change:—

"He hangs in shades the orange bright,

Like golden lamps in a green night."

The emphasis is sometimes placed on the first syllable, as in the subjoined:—

"Fling but a stone—the giant dies."

"Smoothing the rugged brow of night."

The decasyllabic verse, however, will allow more fully of the illustration of the subjects of Accent and Pause.

In the meantime, a word, and only a word, requires to be said regarding verses of nine syllables. Such verses, in their normal and most natural shape, start with two short syllables, followed by a long one; and the same arrangement, repeated twice afterwards successively, completes the line. It has thus but three accented to six unaccented vowel-sounds. Few poets of any repute have used this measure extensively, if we except Shenstone, to whose style it gives an almost unique caste. For example—

"Not a pine in my grove is there seen,

But with tendrils of woodbine is bound;

Not a beech's more beautiful green,

But a sweet-briar entwines it around.

One would think she might like to retire

To the bower I have labour'd to rear;

Not a shrub that I heard her admire,

But I hasted and planted it there."

Shenstone often introduces eight syllables only, as in the following stanza:—

"Ye shepherds, so cheerful and gay,

Whose flocks never carelessly roam,

Should Corydon's happen to stray,

Oh! call the poor wanderers home."

But he here retains the proper rhythm of the measure of nine syllables, and the lines just quoted may rightly be looked on as still in that verse, though defective in a syllable. There are several modes of writing the same measure, different from that of Shenstone, but it may suffice to notice one instance:—

"When in death I shall calmly recline,

Oh bear my heart to my mistress dear;

Tell her it lived upon smiles and wine

Of the brightest hue, while it linger'd here."

These lines are far from being very musical in themselves, and were only so written to suit precomposed music. They are indeed positively harsh, if read without a recollection of that music, and confirm the remark made, that each numerical assemblage or series of syllables appears to have only one kind of rhythm proper and natural to it, and apart from which it is usually immelodious.

The ten-syllabled line is the heroic one of the English language, and a noble one it is, rivalling the lofty hexameter of Greece and Rome, and casting utterly into the shade the dancing, frivolous epic measure of French poetry. The latter runs in this rhythmical fashion:—

"She is far from the land where her young hero sleeps."

And in this measure is composed the "Henriade" of Voltaire, with all the famed tragedies of Corneille and Racine, as well as the pungent satires of Boileau. How characteristic of the Gaul the adoption and use of such a sing-song form of heroic verse! The decasyllabic line of England is of a more dignified caste, while, at the same time, capable of serving far more numerous and varied purposes. "All thoughts, all passions, all delights, whatever stirs this mortal frame," it has been found fitted to give expression to in a manner worthy of the themes. A glorious vehicle it proved for the inspirations of Chaucer, Spenser, Shakspeare, Jonson, Beaumont, Fletcher, Milton, Dryden, Pope, Thomson, Akenside, Young, Goldsmith, Cowper, and other bards of past generations; while scarcely less magnificent has been the handling of the same measure by the poets of the last age, the third great one in our literary annals. Crabbe, Wordsworth, Coleridge, Rogers, Campbell, Southey, Byron, Shelley, and Keats, with other recent poets of deserved renown, have all wielded the decasyllabic line, with or without rhyme, with success, as well as with singularly varied ability. A long list of dramatists of the Elizabethan, Annean, and Georgean eras, has of course to be added to the roll now given.

The heroic or epic measure of English verse consists of ten-syllabled lines, each of which, in its ordinary rhythmical form, presents a short and long syllable alternately. The length of the line enables us distinctly to trace in it both accent and pause; and it is upon frequent changes in the seats of these that the varied harmony of the heroic measure depends. The general accentuation falls on the long syllables, the sense, however, always directing the reader to accent some single syllable specially in each line. The pause uniformly follows the syllable or word so accented specially, unless that syllable be the first part of a long word, or be followed by short monosyllables. Thus, in the following lines the accent is severed from the pause.[26] Both are marked:—

"As bu´sy—as intentive emmets are."

"So fresh the wou´nd is—and the grief so vast."

"Those seats of lu´xury—debate and pride."

The pause is usually marked by a comma or period, but this, as before said, is not necessarily the case. In reading the decasyllabic line, a pause must somewhere be made, whether or not the sense be divided by points of any kind. The writings of Pope exemplify strikingly the formal or normal rhythm, accent, and pause of the heroic line, and a quotation may be made to exhibit these fully. The pause is marked in each line, and the same mark shows the seat of the accent:—

"Here as I watch'd´ the dying lamps around,

From yonder shrine´ I heard a hollow sound.

Come, sister, come´! (it said, or seem'd to say)

Thy place is here´; sad sister, come away;

Once like thyself´, I trembled, wept, and pray'd,

Love's victim then´, though now a sainted maid:

But all is calm´ in this eternal sleep;

Here grief forgets to groan´, and love to weep;

Even superstition´ loses every fear,

For God, not man´, absolves our frailties here."

This passage contains the secret of that smoothness which so peculiarly characterises the versification of Pope. In the preceding fourteen lines, the accent and the pause are seated, in all save three instances, at the same or fourth syllable; or rather the seat of the accent is only once altered (at the twelfth line), while the pause, changed there, is also changed in the fourth and thirteenth lines, where it occurs on the fifth and short syllables in the words "echoes" and "superstition," the accent remaining on the fourth in both cases. Now, the versification of Pope is by no means so monotonous at all times, but it is sufficiently marked by the peculiar features exhibited here—that is, the reiterated location of the accent and pause near the middle of each line, with the pause most frequently at long syllables—to render his verses smooth even to a wearisome excess. It is this characteristic of structure, often felt but seldom understood, which distinguishes the poetry of Pope from that of almost every other writer of note in the language. Darwin resembles him most closely, though the latter poet had marked peculiarities of his own. He emphasised more particularly nearly one-half the first syllables of his lines. Verse after verse runs thus:—

"Sighs in the gale, and whispers in the grot."

"Spans the pale nations with colossal stride."

The sweetness here is great, but, most undoubtedly, verse possessed of a much more perfect and uncloying species of melody has been produced by those poets who have admitted greater variety into the composition of their lines. The licence used by Shakspeare, for example, in respect of rhythm, accent, and pause, is unlimited; and beautiful, indeed, are the results:—

"The quality of mercy´ is not strain'd.

It droppeth´ as the gentle dew from heaven

Upon the place beneath´. It is twice bless'd:

It blesseth him that gives´, and him that takes;

'Tis mightiest in the mightiest´; it becomes

The throned monarch´ better than his crown;

It is an attribute´ to God himself."

"Sweet´ are the uses of adversity,

Which, like a toad´, ugly and venomous,

Wears yet a precious jewel´ in his head."

"I know a bank´ whereon the wild thyme blows,

Where oxlips´ and the nodding violet grows,

Quite over-canopied´ with lush woodbine,

With sweet musk-ro´ses, and with eglantine."

It is unnecessary to multiply examples of this sort. The decasyllabic line of Shakspeare is varied in structure, as said, almost unlimitedly, the seat of the accent and pause being shifted from the first word to the last, as if at random, but often, in reality, with a fine regard to the sense. Ben Jonson, and indeed all our older writers, indulge in the like free variations of the heroic measure; and the poets of the present day, in imitating their higher qualities, have also followed their example in respect of mere versification. Wordsworth and Keats, perhaps, may be held as having excelled all the moderns, their contemporaries, in the *art* of "building the lofty rhyme." Both attended specially to the subject, deeming it by no means beneath them to meditate well the melody of single lines, and the aptitude even of individual words. Hence may Coleridge justly praise Wordsworth for "his austere purity of language," and "the perfect appropriateness of his words to the meaning"—for his "sinewy strength" in isolated verses, and "the frequent *curiosa felicitas* of his diction." But Wordsworth himself owns his artistic care and toil in composition even more strongly:—

"When happiest fancy has inspired the strains,

How oft the malice of one luckless word

Pursues the Enthusiast to the social board,

Or haunts him lated on the silent plains!"

The beauties of the Bard of Rydal are, at the same time, too widely spread to render him the best example for our present purpose. Keats attended more closely to the minutiæ of pure versification in single passages, and may furnish better illustrations here. The subjoined Arcadian picture displays exquisite ease and freedom of composition:—

"Leading the way´, young damsels danced along,

Bearing the burden´ of a shepherd's song;

Each having a white wicker´, overbrimm'd

With April's tender younglings´; next well trimm'd,

A crowd of shepherds´ with as sunburn'd looks

As may be read of´ in Arcadian books;

Such´ as sat listening round Apollo's pipe.

When the great deity´, for earth too ripe,

Let his divinity´ o'erflowing die

In music through the vales of Thessaly."

Equally fine is the varied melody of the young poet's blank verse:—

"As when´, upon a trancèd summer night,

Those green-robed senators´ of mighty woods,

Tall oaks´, branch-charmèd by the earnest stars,

´ Dream', and so dream all night without a stir,

Save from one gradual´ solitary gust

Which comes upon the silence´, and dies off,

As if the ebbing air´ had but one wave;

So came these words and went."

Before adverting to other characters and peculiarities of English Versification generally, a very few words may be said in reference to those measures that exceed the decasyllabic in length. Lines of eleven feet have never been used in the composition of great or extended poems. When employed in lyrics and occasional pieces, the rhythm has usually been thus regulated:—

"Oh! breathe not his name, let it sleep in the shade,

Where, cold and unhonour'd, his relics are laid;

Sad, silent, and dark be the tears which we shed

As (the) night-dew that falls on the grass o'er his head."

This rhythmical arrangement seems to be the natural one, and composes merely the normal line of nine syllables, with a prefix of two others. Some other forms of the eleven-syllabled line may be found in lyrical collections, and more particularly in the works of Thomas Moore, who, writing to pre-existing music, has produced specimens of almost every variety of rhythm of which the English language is capable.

The measure of twelve syllables has been employed by one eminent and true poet in the composition of a work of importance. The "Polyolbian" of Drayton is here alluded to. As in the case of other verses of an even number of syllables, the regular alternation of short and long seems most suitable to lines of twelve. Drayton thought so, as the following brief extract descriptive of Robin Hood will show:—

"Then, taking them to rest, his merry men and he

Slept many a summer's night beneath the greenwood tree.

From wealthy abbots' chests, and churls' abundant store,

What oftentimes he took he shared among the poor;

No lordly bishop came in lusty Robin's way,

To him before he went, but for his pass must pay;

The widow in distress he graciously relieved,

And remedied the wrongs of many a virgin grieved."

It is superfluous to dwell on accentuation or pauses here, the line being commonly divided into two even parts, or, in truth, two six-syllabled lines. The rhythm, however, is often arranged differently in lyrics, as the first lines of some of those of Moore will evince:—

"As a beam o'er the face of the waters may glow."

"We may roam through this world like a child at a feast."

"Like the bright lamp that shone in Kildare's holy fane."

In these instances, two short syllables and a long one occur in alternation throughout the twelve. Moore has given other varieties of this measure, as—

"Through grief and through danger, thy smile hath cheer'd my way;"

but these are merely capriccios to suit certain music, and need not occupy our time here. The same poet has even a line of thirteen syllables.[27]

"At the mid-hour of night, when stars are weeping I fly."

This measure is a most awkward one, certainly. The line of fourteen syllables is more natural, and was used in at least one long piece called

"Albion's England," by Thomas Warner, a rhymer of the sixteenth century. A maid is advised whom to love in these terms:—

"The ploughman's labour hath no end, and he a churl will prove;

The craftsman hath more work on hand than fitteth one to love;

The merchant trafficking abroad, suspects his wife at home;

A youth will play the wanton, and an old will play the mome:

Then choose a shepherd."

This is but the lumbering dodecasyllabic verse rendered more lumbering still by two fresh feet, it will be generally allowed. In fact, these lines of twelve and fourteen feet have only been used effectually as "Alexandrines," or single lines introduced to wind up, or heighten the force of passages, in the heroic or the octosyllabic measure. Pope ridicules this practice, though it was a favourite one with Dryden:—

"A needless Alexandrine ends the song,

That, like a wounded snake, drags its slow length along."

In Dryden's "Ode to music," the following instances of the two kinds of Alexandrines occur:—

"Could swell the soul to rage, or kindle soft desire."

"And thrice he routed all his foes, and thrice he slew the slain."

By giving lines of ten, twelve, and fourteen syllables in succession, as he occasionally does in his translation of Virgil, Dryden brings passages with artistic skill to a very noble climax. But the Alexandrine is now nearly obsolete in our poetry.

The most common features and peculiarities of English Versification have now received a share of attention. Measure and Rhythm,—Accent and Pause, have all been duly noticed. There are yet other points, however, connected with the subject, which merit equal attention from the student of poetical composition. Every rule that has been mentioned may be preserved, and still most inharmonious verse may be the result. The greatest poets, either from experience or innate musical taste, adopted additional means to arrive at perfect versification. Pope points to some of these in his well-known lines:—

"The sound must seem an echo to the sense.

Soft is the strain when zephyr gently blows,

And the smooth stream in smoother numbers flows;

But when loud surges lash the sounding shore,

The hoarse rough verse should like the torrent roar."

The poet, as all will of course see, here exemplifies the meaning of his lines practically in their structure. The Greek and Roman writers were quite aware of the effect of congruous sound and sense. Virgil has several famous lines constructed on this principle, as—

"Monstrum, horrendum, informe, ingens cui lumen ademptum."

(A monster, horrid, formless, gross, and blind.)

To give a better idea of the efficient way in which the poet has roughened the above verse to suit the picture of a monster, one of his ordinary lines may be quoted:—

"Formosam resonare doces Amaryllida silvas."

But it is wrong to call this an ordinary line, since Dr. Johnson considered it to be the most musical in any human language. Ovid, again, has made the sense and sound (and also construction) agree finely in the following passage:—

"Sponte sua carmen numeros veniebat ad aptos,

Et quod tentabam dicere versus erat."

Pope has imitated these lines, and applied them to himself, the signification being simply—

"I lisp'd in numbers, for the numbers came."

Among our own great bards, Milton stands peculiarly distinguished for success in the use of this ornament of verse. The "Allegro" and "Penseroso" exhibit various exquisite instances.

"Swinging slow with sullen roar."

"On the light fantastic toe."

"Through the high wood echoing shrill."

"And the busy hum of men."

"Most musical, most melancholy."

"Lap me in soft Lydian airs."

In the "Paradise Lost," again, there occur many passages rendered forcible in the extreme by the adaptation of sound to sense. Thus—

"Him the Almighty power

Hurl'd headlong flaming from the ethereal sky,

With hideous ruin and combustion, down

To bottomless perdition."

Still more remarkable is the following passage, as expressive of slow and toilsome travel:—

"The fiend

O'er bog or steep, through straight, rough, dense, or rare,

With head, hands, wings, or feet, pursues his way,

And swims, or sinks, or wades, or creeps, or flies."

The chief mean of attaining *general harmony* in verse is *a free and happy distribution of the vowel-sounds*. For producing a *special harmony*, consonant with *special signification*, other rules require to be followed. But, in the first place, let us look particularly to the means of rendering verse simply and aggregately melodious. It must not be supposed, as many are apt to do, that even the most illustrious poets considered it beneath them to attend to such minutiæ as the distribution of the vowels in their verses. Look at the grand opening of "Paradise Lost." It is scarcely conceivable that the remarkable variation of the vowels there, on which the effect will be found largely to depend, can have been the result of chance. No one line almost, it will be seen, gives the same vowel-*sound* twice.

"Of man's first disobedience, and the fruit

Of that forbidden tree, whose mortal taste

Brought death into the world, and all our woe,

With loss of Eden, till one greater Man

Restore us, and regain the heavenly seat,

Sing, heavenly Muse."

The following stanza of Leyden was considered by Scott one of the most musical in the language, and it is rendered so mainly by its vowel variety:—

"How sweetly swell on Jura's heath

The murmurs of the mountain bee!

How sweetly mourns the writhèd shell,

Of Jura's shore, its parent sea!"

A passage from the "Laodamia" of Wordsworth may be pointed to as an equally striking illustration of the same rule:—

"He

Spake of heroic arts in graver mood

Revived, with finer harmony pursued;

Of all that is most beauteous—imaged there

In happier beauty; more pellucid streams,

An ampler ether, a diviner air,

And fields invested with purpureal glaems;

Climes which the sun, who sheds the brightest day

Earth knows, is all unworthy to survey."

Wordsworth, who in truth is the perfect master of this species of Melody, as the "Excursion" will prove to all those who look thereinto attentively, has scarcely once repeated the same exact sound in any two words, of any one line, in the preceding quotation. One more passage (from "Lycidas") may be given to undeceive yet more completely those who have been want to ascribe the rich Miltonic melody to mere chance:—

"Alas! what boots it with incessant care

To tend the homely, slighted shepherd's trade.

And strictly meditate the thankless Muse?

Were it not better done, as others use,

To sport with Amaryllis in the shade,

Or with the tangles of Neæra's hair?"

This most melodious passage has often been quoted, but the source of its melody has not been generally recognised by ordinary readers. The key which unlocks the secret has here been given. Let it be applied to our poetry at large, and it will be found to explain the effect of many of its grandest and sweetest passages.

The proper distribution of the vowels, then, so effective in the hands of Milton and Wordsworth, may be decisively viewed as a main help to harmony of versification generally. But when the poet desires to make his language express *particular* meanings by sounds, he studies more specially, in the first place, the right disposition of accent and pause, and so advances partly to his object. Thus Milton, in describing the fall of Mulciber or Vulcan from heaven, leaves him, as it were, tumbling and tumbling in the verse, by a beautiful pause:—

"From morn

To noon he fell, from noon to dewy eve,

A summer's day."

A similar and not less exquisite pause is made in the famed passage, otherwise beautiful from variety of vowels, where, after swelling allusions to

"What resounds

In fable or romance of Uther's son

Begirt with British and Armoric knights,

And all who since, baptized or infidel,

Jousted in Aspramount or Montalbalm,"

a dying and most melodious close is attained—

"When Charlemain with all his peerage fell

By Fontarabia."

Often are similar pauses made effectively at the opening of lines:—

"The schoolboy, wandering through the wood,

To pull the primrose gay,

Starts, the new voice of spring to hear,

And imitates thy lay."

"My song, its pinions disarray'd of night,

Droop'd."

"The carvèd angels, ever eager eyed,

Stared."

"Liberty,

From heart to heart, from tower to tower, o'er Spain

Scattering contagious fire into the sky,

Gleam'd."

Much more striking instances of the effect of laying marked and compulsory pauses on first syllables might be adduced, but these, taken by chance, may suffice as illustrations. Such aids to impressive versifying must not be overlooked by young poets. The pause and accent, however, may both be similarly employed and fixed without the help of positive periods. Thus Wordsworth, in lines likewise beautiful from vowel-variety:—

"What time the hunter's earliest horn is heard,

Startling the golden hills."

The voice accents the word "startling" naturally; and mind and ear both own its peculiar aptitude where it is placed. Not less marked is the force of the same word in the middle of the Miltonic line:—

"To hear the lark begin his flight,

And singing *startle* the dull night."

And again, in the case of the word "start"—

"The patriot nymph *starts* at imagined sounds."

The following are examples of sense brought clearly out, by placing the pause and accent at different points of the verses:—

"My heart *aches*, and a drowsy numbness pains

My sense."

"Cut mercy with a sharp *knife* to the bone."

The strong effect of these lines arises from the accent being thrown on syllables usually short or unaccented in the decasyllabic verse. This is a common stroke of art with Milton, when he would lay force on particular words. Most of our great poets, indeed, knew and practised the same rule.

So much for the effects of the structure of the verse, and the location of the accent and pause. But the simple choice of *apt diction* is still more important to the art of effective versification, as far as the evolution of special meanings is concerned. Reference is not here made to diction that is apt through signification merely, but such, more particularly, as by its *sound* enhances the force of the thoughts or images which it conveys. In this shape is the congruity of sound and sense best developed. To the instances given from Pope and Milton others may now be added, with an explanation of the artistic rules employed in the case.

Observe how finely appropriate is the sound to the sense in the line:—

"The surgy murmurs of the lonely sea."

By the use of the *rs* here it is, that the very sound of the surge seems to be brought to the ear; and even the open vowels at the close give something like the sense of a great and cold waste of waters beyond the surge. Equally apt is the impression made by the lines:—

"The murmurous haunt of flies on summer-eves."

"Couches of rugged stone, and slaty ridge

Stubborn'd with iron."

"A ghostly under-song,

Like hoarse night-gusts sepulchral briars among."

"The snorting of the war-horse of the storm."

These are instances in which the roughening effect of the *r* is felt to aid the meaning powerfully. The actual and direct meaning of the words chosen, beyond a doubt, is by far the most important point in all kinds of composition; but the art of the poet may be more or less evinced in his selection of such as have a fit and correspondent sound. All great poets have recognised this law. The art, however, must not be too palpable. Pope, in exemplifying the harsh effect of the letter *r*, allowed the art to be too easily seen.

"The hoarse rough verse should like the torrent roar."

Keats, before quoted, manages the matter more delicately.

We refer to the use of the letter *r* simply in illustration of a principle of great consequence in poetical composition. It is also of the widest application. Not a letter, or combination of letters, in the English language, is without some peculiar force of sound of its own, enhancing sense; and above all does this assertion hold good in respect to the Anglo-Saxon elements or portions of our vernacular tongue. This circumstance arises from the fact of the Anglo-Saxon being a very pure dialect of a primitive language, the earliest words of which languages are ever mere descriptions, as far as sound goes, of the acts or objects implied or spoken of. *Hiss* and *howl*, for instance, are clearly imitative of the noises of hissing and howling; and thousands of similarly derived vocables are not less expressive in a kindred way. Our most eminent national poets, whether taught by the ear or by experience, have shown themselves well aware of these things, and have turned to fine account the Anglo-Saxon constituents of the mother-tongue. In those languages, again, which have passed through various shapes since their first invention by man—as the French, Spanish, and Italian—nearly all traces of congruous sound and sense have been lost, and general modulation has taken place of specific expressiveness. The gain here, which practically rests on the use of a multiplicity of vowels, cannot be held to counterbalance the loss. Exquisitely melodious as are the verses of Tasso and Ariosto, for example, no one wholly ignorant of Italian could ever even guess at the meaning of a single line or word from the mere hearing. The English language stands placed, in the main, very differently: and happily does it do so, as far as force, impressiveness, and picturesque beauty are concerned. No doubt, we have many words founded on the Latin and its modern derivations; and these are far from unserviceable, inasmuch as they lend general harmony to our tongue, spoken and written. But our special strength of diction comes from the Anglo-Saxon; and fortunate is it, that that primitive form of speech still forms the chief constituent of the national language of Britain.

The reader now understands by what means our best national poets have striven to render sound and sense congruous in their verses. It has mainly been, as said, by the use of Anglo-Saxon words which could scarcely fail to suit the end well, since they were actually formed, primarily, upon that very principle. Much of the power, of course, lies in the consonants which occur so freely in the language; and yet the vowels, while essential to the use and force of the consonants, are not without their individual and respective kinds and shades of expressiveness. The *o*, for instance, has a breadth and weight not pertaining to the other vowels, as in the last of these two lines—

"Some words she spake

In solemn tenour and deep organ tone."

The other vowels have also their respective degrees of depth, lightness, and other qualities. But mere general harmony only, or chiefly, can be attained by the use of vowel-sounds unaided by consonants of particular powers; and it has already been pointed out, that, to develop that harmony fully, an extensive variation of the said sounds is the principal thing required, and has ever been employed by the greatest poets.

With regard to Consonants, there is scarcely one in the alphabet without some well-marked and special force of its own. By conjunction with others, or with vowels, this special force may likewise be modified vastly, giving rise to numberless varieties of expression, or rather expressiveness. The roughening power of the letter *r* has been adverted to, and other consonants may now be noticed, with exemplifications, of their efficient use in poetry. The consonants are noticeable for their peculiar powers, at once at the beginning, in the middle, and at the close of words; but the present purpose will be best served by taking them up successively, as initial letters.

The consonant *b*, at the opening of words, has no very marked force; but it originates many expressive terms, often finely employed in poetry.

"He *babbled* of green fields."

Here the word paints the act to perfection. "*Beslubbered* all with tears." "A *blubbering* boy." "Fire burn, and caldron *bubble*." All of these words exemplify sound and sense clearly combined; and our poets have also used, with like effect, *bawl*, *brawl*, *bray*, and many other common terms, beginning with *b*. But on the whole, its initial power is not great; and it is, indeed, rather a soft consonant, like the labials generally. *C*, again, sounded as *k*, has really a special power, quick, sharp, and cutting, at the commencement of words, and more particularly when followed by *l* and *r*, and aided by apt terminations. Well did Milton and others of our bards know this fact, as the subjoined lines may partly show:—

"*Clash'd* their sounding shields the din of war."

"Till all his limbs do *crack*."

"I *cleave* with rapid fin the wave."

"In one wild havoc *crash'd*."

"The moonbeams *crisp* the *curling* surge."

"By the howling of the dog."

"By the *croaking* of the frog."

All these are effective terms, both in the opening and close. Those who recollect any great actor in "Hamlet," must have noticed the splendid emphasis placeable on the words—

"What should such fellows as I do,

Crawling betwixt earth and heaven!"

The following is most aptly heavy:—

"Save that a *clog* doth hang yet at my heel."

And we have here a fine expression, with an equally good pause:—

"I plead a pardon for my tale,

And having hemmed and *cough'd*—begin."

But *cough* must be pronounced in the old Anglo-Saxon way, and not as *coff*. The power of the letter *d*, at the commencement of words, is not quick and sharp like the *c*, but rather slow and heavy; and this effect is vastly increased when an *r* is added. Thus, for instance:—

"*Drags* its slow length along."

"Not all the *drowsy* syrups of the world."

"The *dreary* melody of bedded reeds."

"Snivelling and *drivelling* folly without end."

"Good shepherds after shearing *drench* their sheep."

"And *dropping* melody with every tear."

Such words, too, as *drawl, droop, drip, drizzle, drum*, and others, may be, have been used excellently in poetry. The *f* is a letter expressive of a light and rapid action, at least when conjoined with other consonants. Campbell uses it finely in both ways:—

"But see! 'mid the *fast-flashing* lightnings of war.

What steed to the desert *flies frantic and far?*"

The quick action is also signified in *flay*, *flog*, *fling*, *flitter*, and other vocables. Coriolanus portrays verbally the very deed, when he tells how,

"Like an eagle in a dovecot, he

Flutter'd their Volsces in Corioli."

G, by itself, is rather a soft consonant; and, followed by *l*, it has also a mild effect, as in the very expressive words, *gleam*, *glide*, *glitter*, *glisten*, *gloom*, and the like. *Gr*, again, is singularly heavy and harsh, as in the succeeding cases:——

"And *grinn'd*, terrific, a sardonic look."

"*Grinn'd* horribly a ghastly smile."

"*Grapple* him to thy soul with hooks of steel."

"In came Margaret's *grimly* ghost."

Of kindred force are *grasp*, *gripe*, *grope*, and others. *Gnash* and *gnaw* have a sort of convulsive twist in sense, and so should they have in sound, when rightly pronounced, and after the original mode. By the way, though *grin* be a strong word, in its old shape it is stronger; and that *girn*, still used in Scotland.

All of these specimens of the Anglo-Saxon vocabulary, and many of a kindred order, have been often made to tell exquisitely in our national poetry. The same averment may be made regarding hosts of other words, differently begun and formed; but we must so far content ourselves with having shown the principle, and go over what is to come more quickly. However, the aspirate *h* must not be lightly overpassed, having a striking value in verse. Being pronounced with an *aspiration*, it gives a certain energy to almost all words which it begins, as *hack*, *harsh*, *hawl*, *haste*, *hit*, *hunt*, and the like. To some terms it imparts a sort of laboriously *elevative* force. Pope composed the following line purposely to exemplify this property:——

Up the high hill, he heaves a huge round stone."

The merely expiratory force of the *h* is felt equally in naming the "heights of heaven" and the "hollows of hell." Though but half a letter, it is thus potent in poetry, and is often beautifully turned to account by Milton, as in the passage, "Him the Almighty power *hurled headlong*," and so on.

The letter *j* gives the initiative to many expressive words, though their expressiveness rests mainly on the terminations. Such is the case with *jar*, *jerk*, *jig*, *jilt*, *jog*, *jostle*, *jumble*, *jump*. Our comic writers have used the most of these to good purpose. It is worth while specially to notice *jeer*. It would seem as if the *eer* was an ending peculiarly fitted to express the meaning which *jeer* bears, since it gives a pretty similar force to *sneer*, *fleer*, *leer*, *peer*, *queer*, and some others. Sound and sense concur in all these terms. The *k* merely gives to words the same power as the hard *c*. L has no great force as the initial letter of words, though it yet possesses so far its own peculiar expressiveness. That the whole members of the alphabet do so, indeed, may be very simply proved. Of the following twelve monosyllables closing in *ash*, the different opening letters give a different force, in respect of sound, to each word, and such as perfectly accords with the actual and several meanings. The words are, *clash*, *crash*, *dash*, *flash*, *gnash*, *lash*, *mash*, *quash*, *plash*, *slash*, *smash*, and *thrash*. The distinction here may not be great in some instances, but it certainly is so in the grating *crash*, the rapid *flash*, and the ponderous *smash*! These points are well worthy the attention of the student of English Versification—in truth, of English literature generally.

Many expressive words, opening with *l*, are formed by apt closes, as *lift*, *lisp*, *limp*, *loathe*, *log*, *lull*, and *lurk*. How fine the *loll* in Shakspeare's line:—

"The large Achilles, on his press'd bed *lolling*,

From his deep chest laughs out a loud applause!"

M and *n*, opening words isolatedly, have little peculiarity of power, but gain it by continuations and terminations:—

"Hell is *murky*."

"To pluck the *mangled* Tybalt from his shroud."

"Thrice the brinded cat hath *mew'd*."

"The *matted* woods."

"Thou detestable womb, thou *maw* of death."

"So the two brothers and their *murder'd* man."

"This hand is *moist*, my lady."

"The *muffled* drum."

And so on. *Neigh, nod, nip, nick* and so forth, exemplify the *n* sufficiently. There are fewer words of a very expressive kind opened by *p*, than by any other letter which may be followed by other consonants, as *l* and *r*. Nor need *q* delay our progress. R, however, as already observed, is one of the most emphatic letters in the alphabet; and, whether at the beginning, in the middle, or at the close of words, it gives them a striking and specific force in enunciation. Rude and rough power lies in its sound. The monosyllabic verbs which it commences show well what its original effect was felt to be. *Race, rage, rack, rail, rain, rake, ramp, range, rant, rate, rave, rash, raze*—all these words have an affinity of meaning, derived from the *ra*, though modified by the endings. Followed by other vowels, the *r* softens somewhat, as in *reach, reap, ride, rise*, and the like; but still there is force of action implied in the sound. *Ring, rip*, and *rift*, may be styled *ear-pictures*. It is impossible, by citations, to give any conception of the extent to which the *r* has been used in imparting fitting emphasis to poetry. Nearly all words, implying terror or horror, rest mainly on it for their picturesque force. This point, however, has been already illustrated sufficiently for the present purpose.

S, by itself, opens many words of mild action, as *sail, sew, sit, soar*, and *suck*. With an additional consonant; *sc, sh, sk, sl, sm, sn, sp, sq, st*, and *su* it gives rise to most potent verbs of action; and still stronger ones are formed when another consonant is added, as in the cases of *scr, spr*, and *str*. What is chiefly to the point here, sense and sound are strikingly congruous in terms of this formation. The initials give force whatever the endings may be, though these may modify it largely. Let the reader look well at the following list. *Scald, scalp, scare, scamper, scatter, scoff, scorn, scowl, scour, scourge, scrape, scrawl, scratch, scream, screw, scrub, scramble, scraggy, scud; shake, shape, shave, shift, shine, shirk, shiver, shock, shoot, shout, shriek, shrill, shrink, shrug, shuffle, shudder, skate, skim, skiff, skirr; slap, slay, sleep, slumber, slip, slit, slink, sling, slow, slough, sluggish, slur, slut, sly; smash, smite, smile, smooth, smug, smuggle, smother; snap, snarl, snare, snatch, snib, snip, snub, sneap, snack, snort, snivel, snell; speed, spit, split, splash, spout, spring, spur, spurt, spurn, sputter, spy, sprinkle; squeeze, squall, squeak, squat, squash, squabble, squib; stab, stamp, stare, start, steal, steam, steep, steer, step, stem, stick, sting, stir, stoop, storm, stow; strain, strap, streak, stress, stretch, strew, stride, strike, string, strip,* strive, stroll, strut, stuff, stump, stun, stagger, stammer, *startle, strangle, stutter, struggle, stumble; sway, sweep, swell, swing, swoop, swirl.*

This is truly a long roll; but it is one deserving of all attention from those who are studying the euphony, or the happy cacophony, of the English vocabulary, with an eye to poetic composition. Each word here is, to repeat a somewhat dubious phrase, a positive auricular picture. There is variety in sense, but it is still accompanied by fit variety of sound. And yet a general similarity of significations exists among the words formed by *s* with one or more additional consonants: while still more akin are the sets of words begun alike. The whole, collectively, express force, and for the most part strong force. *Scare* and *scream* imply (in sound and sense) sharp action; *shake* and *shrink*, soft and moderate; *skate* and *skim*, quick and smooth; *slip* and *sling*, rapid and easy; *smash* and *smite*, strong and suppressive; *snarl* and *snap*, snarling and snappish; *spit* and *split*, slight but decisive; *squeeze* and *squeak*, forcible but petty; *stab* and *stamp*, direct and powerful; *strain* and *strike*, full of *straining strength*, and with their congeners, the most energetic of words, in sound and sense, in the language. In verbs opened by *sw*, as in *sweep* and *swirl*, the *s* gives an onward impulse, as it were, and the *w* renders it so far rotatory. Leigh Hunt applies the word swirl finely to ships:—

"They chase the whistling brine, and swirl into the bay."

Most of the words formed with *t* as the initial derive from it no very marked force, and depend for that quality on the same terminations which have been noticed as giving force to others. The *t* need not, therefore, occupy our space. The *w* is also weak alone, but forms terms of some initial pith with the aspirate *h* as *wheel*, *whiff*, *whelm*, *whip*, *whirl*, *whisk*, and *whoop*. There is a sort of sense of circuitous motion given by the *wh*; and, with their well-discriminated terminations, the verbs of action which it opens are very expressive. When *wr* was pronounced *uurr*, the words, *wrangle*, *wrestle*, *wreath*, *wring*, *wrench*, and *wrath* were words of potency, twisting and convulsive. But the *w* is now mute, and their might has departed.

It is because much, very much, of the power, the majesty, and the beauty of English Poetry, as left to us by our fathers, is traceable to the liberal use of the Anglo-Saxon elements of our national language, that the subject has been treated of here so lengthily. Moreover, there has been evinced of late, it is painful to add, a growing tendency on the part of many writers to cultivate Gallicisms, as words of Roman derivation are rightly named, to a still greater extent than has yet been done amongst us, and to the repression of our true native vocabulary. A gain may be made in this way in respect of general harmony, as before observed, but it is a gain which never can counterbalance the loss in point of pith and picturesqueness. It is not said here, that our greater recent poets have been the chief deserters of the Anglo-Saxon tongue. On the contrary, many of them have shown a full sense of its merits, and have used it finely. It is a remarkable corroboration, indeed, of the present argument, that in all their best passages, they almost uniformly employ the said tongue, whether consciously or unconsciously. Look at the following passage of Burns. It has been pronounced by critics to embody the most powerful picture in modern poetry.

"Coffins stood round like open presses,

That shaw'd the dead in their last dresses;

And by some devilish cantrip sleight,

Each in its cauld hand held a light,

By which heroic Tam was able

To note upon the haly table

A murderer's banes in gibbet-airns;

Twa span-lang, wee unchristen'd bairns;

A thief, new cuttit frae a rape—

Wi' his last gasp his gab did gape;

A garter which a babe had strangled;

A knife, a father's throat had mangled,

Whom his ain son o' life had reft—

The gray hairs yet stack to the heft."

This passage forms a splendid specimen of almost pure Anglo-Saxon; and, among the few words of a different origin, one of the most marked may perhaps be rightly held a blemish—namely *heroic*. Like Burns, Wordsworth, and all those moderns who have studied ear-painting (if this phrase may be again pardoned) as well as eye-painting in their verses, have drawn freely on the Anglo-Saxon vocabulary. All young and incipient versifiers should study their works, and "Go and do likewise."

The general construction of English verse, and the various rules by which it is rendered melodious, expressive, and picturesque, having now been explained, it remains but to indicate, in a few words, the principal divisions of Poetry common, among us. Epic verse is held to be the highest description of poetical composition. The "Iliad" of Homer and "Æneid" of Virgil have always formed models in this department; and it is remarkable, but true, that we can scarcely be said to have one English epic that rises to their standard, saving "Paradise Lost." Of the character of an epic, it need but be said here, that the subject, the diction, and the treatment must all be alike lofty and sustained. In English, the decasyllabic is the epic line, sometimes called the Heroic. If we have so few epics, however, we have many poems of high note that are usually styled Didactic, from their *teaching* great truths. Akenside, Thomson, Cowper, Rogers, and Campbell wrote such poems, some in blank verse, others in rhyme. Where rhymed, they are all written in Couplets, or pairs of lines, rhyming to one another, in regular succession. Narrative, Descriptive, and Satiric poems (the several objects of which may be drawn from these epithets) are important species of composition, and for the most part constructed similarly to the Epic and Didactic pieces. In truth, the ten-syllabled line, in couplets or in blank verse, though best adapted for grave subjects, has been employed on almost all themes by English poets. Nearly the same thing may be said of the octosyllabic verse, also written commonly in couplets, when used in long compositions. Many poems, which may be generally termed Romantic, have likewise been framed in the eight-syllabled line, though not usually in couplets.

The name of Stanzas is bestowed, aggregately, on all assemblages of lines, exceeding two in number, when they are arranged continuously. The following is a stanza of three lines, termed isolatedly a Triplet:—

"Nothing, thou elder brother even to Shade.

Thou hadst a being ere the world was made,

And (well fix'd) art alone of ending not afraid."

Stanzas in four lines, called specially Quatrains, are exemplified in Gray's "Churchyard Elegy." Indeed, that stanza has long been denominated the Elegiac. Tennyson's "In Memoriam" is composed in octosyllabic quatrains. In stanzas of four lines, also, half the minor poetry in the language is composed. The general name of "Lyrical" is given to such poetry, and implies the subjects to be occasional and detached, and the pieces usually brief. "Songs" come within the Lyric category. It would be needless to exemplify a stanza so well known, either in its frequent form of alternate rhyming lines of eight and eight syllables, or its yet more common one of eight and six. No continuous poems of any length or moment have been written in five-line stanzas, and few in those of six lines. The latest piece in the latter shape has been Sir E. L. Bulwer's "King Arthur;" but the stanza is too like the very famous one called in Italy the *ottava rima*, with two lines lopped off and not beneficially. The "Don Juan" of Byron is composed in this *ottava rima*, or eight-lined stanza; but it was borrowed from the Italians (the real inventors) by William Tennant, and used in his "Anster Fair," long before Frere or Byron thought of its appropriation—a circumstance of which many critics have shown a discreditable ignorance. It is the best of all stanzas for a light or burlesque epic, the principle of its construction being—seriousness in the first six lines, and in the last two a mockery of that seriousness. The great poet, however, can make any stanza great. Shakspeare used the six-line stanza in his "Venus and Adonis," and that of seven lines in his "Lucrece."

The only other regular English stanza, of high note, and calling for mention here, is the Spenserian, consisting of nine lines, the first eight decasyllabic, and the last an Alexandrine of twelve feet. Many noble poems have been written in this stanza, from Spenser's "Fairy Queen" to Byron's "Childe Harold," which may be viewed as romantic and narrative epics respectively. It is calculated to convey aptly the loftiest poetry, though Thomson and Shenstone have employed it for lighter purposes, in the "Castle of Indolence" and "Schoolmistress."

The sonnet is, in its highest moods, an epic in fourteen lines; and, as regards its normal structure, should present but four different rhymes in all. So Milton wrote it, and so often Wordsworth, *facile principes* in this walk of poetic composition; but six or more rhymes are commonly admitted. The rhymes of the successive lines stand thus, in the Miltonic sonnet:—"arms, seize, please, harms, charms, these, seas, warms, bower, spare, tower, air, power, bare." In a sonnet, Wordsworth splendidly exemplifies the sonnet, and tells its uses and its history. ("Scorn not," &c. Wordsworth's Miscellaneous Sonnets.)

The Ode is a poem of irregular construction, or rather was so constructed by the Greek bard Pindar, and after him by Dryden and Collins, his best English imitators. Wordsworth and Coleridge also wrote fine odes of late years, and they followed the same irregularities of composition. Shelley and Keats, however, produced noble pieces, of the same kind, as those on "Liberty" and "Melancholy," in which they used a very free measure, but in orderly stanzas. It would be out of place to describe at length the plan of the Pindaric ode—for it had a general plan, though fantastic in details. The wildest forms of it were styled the dithyrambic; and impassioned grandeur of sentiment and diction were its characteristics. Horace, in his best odes, contented himself with aiming at dignity and justness of thoughts, and pointedness of expression. Dryden and Collins, as well as Coleridge and Shelley, copied and approached the dithyrambic fervour; while Keats sought but after beauty, and left us masterpieces in that kind—"alas, too few!"

With yet a word on the art of Song-Writing, this essay may be closed. It well merits a word, and chiefly because it is an art the most easy in seeming, and the most difficult in reality, in the entire range of literary composition. People might easily discern this truth, if they would but take note how few really great song-writers have ever flourished among men, at any time, or in any country. Without forgetting Ramsay, Hogg, and Cunningham, it may be justly asserted that Scotland has seen but one such bard, Robert Burns. Ireland has likewise produced but one, Thomas Moore. England has given birth to—not one song-writer of the same high order! Such is the fact; for to such parties as the Dibdins, Charles Morris, or Haynes Bayly, the rank of great song-writers cannot be assigned. However, it is but fair to admit that Moore should be reckoned as in the main a song-writer of England, his music only, and occasionally his subjects, being Irish. His pieces are wholly in the English tongue, and by the English nation he may so far be claimed. That numberless individuals have written one or two good songs, is unquestionable, but the circumstance only strengthens the present argument. It shows the difficulty of fitly carrying out and sustaining the practice of song-writing.

Notwithstanding these glaring truths, the young, on feeling the first prompting of the muse, fly to this species of composition almost invariably. Now, whether they do or do not possess the requisite poetical powers (which is not the point under consideration here), they certainly take up the said task, almost always, in total ignorance of the rules of construction necessary to be observed in song-writing. These are few, but all-important. After simplicity and concentration of thought and diction—the first elements in such compositions—simplicity of grammatical arrangement stands next in consequence. An inverted expression is most injurious, and a parenthetic clause almost uniformly fatal. All forms of complication are indeed alike hurtful; and even epithets, and adjectives of every kind, can be employed but sparingly, and must be most direct and simple. That mode of poetic diction, which introduces its similitudes by "as the," "so the," and "like the," is ruinous in songs. Scarcely less so are interjections, especially when of some length. Look how sadly even Wordsworth failed, when he thought to improve on the old ballad of Helen of Kirkconnel!

"Fair Ellen Irvine, *when, she sate*

Upon the braes of Kirtle,

Was lovely *as a Grecian maid,*

Adorn'd with wreaths of myrtle."

Compare the effect of this stanza with its parenthetic clause and its tale-tagged similitude, to that of the old ballad, so remarkable for its simplicity:—

"I wish I were where Helen lies;

Night and day on me she cries;

Oh! that I were where Helen lies,

On fair Kirkconnel lea."

* * * * * *

"Curst be the head that thought the thought,

Curst be the hand that shot the shot,

When in my arms burd Helen dropt,

And died to succour me."

Even on a reading, the effect of these pieces is widely different, and would be felt ten times more were they sung. The best music is ever cast away on involved phraseology; and herein lies, in fact, the main reason for simplicity of construction in songs.

With these hints on the Art of composing Songs, most of the suggestions before given respecting the selection of words of peculiar sounds, may also be kept in mind. Burns forgot them not. Observe his Wandering Willie:—

"Rest, ye wild winds, in the caves of your slumbers,

How your dread howling a lover alarms."

But let all the most admired songs of Burns, and of Moore also, be examined attentively, and the skilful adaptation of the words to the sentiment, the position and the purpose will appear clearly. What language, for example, could be more artistically suited to an exquisitely soft air than the following by Moore?—

"'Tis the last rose of summer,

Left blooming alone,

All its lovely companions

Are faded and gone."

If these lines were written in a dialect utterly strange to the hearer, he still could not but feel their admirable melodiousness, so appropriate to the melodious music. In the case, therefore, of song-writing generally— whether to known or unknown music—the purpose of the composition must ever be kept in mind. A song, if not satisfactorily fitted for vocal utterance, and intelligible on the hearing of a moment, neither deserves, nor will receive, popular appreciation and acceptance. Where true poetry is interfused, as in the productions of Burns and Moore, then, indeed, is mastership in the art of song-writing really shown. Of all classes of writers, the song-writer is perhaps the most truly an artist.

Rules for Making English Verse.

By EDWARD BYSSHE.

These rules I have, according to the best of my judgment, endeavoured to extract from the practice, and to frame after the examples, of the poets that are most celebrated for a fluent and numerous turn of verse.

In the English versification there are two things chiefly to be considered:

    1. The verses.

    2. The several sorts of poems, or composition in verse.

But because in the verses there are also two things to be observed, the structure of the verse and the rhyme, this treatise shall be divided into three chapters;

    I. Of the structure of English verses.

    II. Of rhyme.

    III. Of the several sorts of poems, or composition in verse.

CHAPTER I.

OF THE STRUCTURE OF ENGLISH VERSES.

The structure of our verses, whether blank or in rhyme, consists in a certain number of syllables; not in feet composed of long and short syllables, as the verses of the Greeks and Romans. And though some ingenious persons formerly puzzled themselves in prescribing rules for the quantity of English syllables, and, in imitation of the Latins, composed verses by the measure of spondees, dactyls, &c., yet the success of their undertaking has fully evinced the vainness of their attempt, and given ground to suspect they had not thoroughly weighed what the genius of our language would bear, nor reflected that each tongue has its peculiar beauties, and that what is agreeable and natural to one, is very often disagreeable, nay, inconsistent with another. But that design being now wholly exploded, it is sufficient to have mentioned it.

Our verses, then, consist in a certain number of syllables; but the verses of double rhyme require a syllable more than those of single rhyme. Thus in a poem whose verses consist of ten syllables, those of the same poem that are accented on the last save one, which we call verses of double rhyme, must have eleven, as may be seen by these verses:—

"A Man so various that he seem'd to be

Not one, but all Mankind's Epitome:

Stiff in Opinion, always in the Wrong,

Was ev'ry thing by starts, and nothing long;

But, in the Course of our revolving moon:

Was Fiddler, Chymist, Statesman and Buffoon:

Then all for Women, Painting, Rhyming, Drinking,

Besides Ten thousand Freaks that dy'd in Thinking,

Praising and Railing were his usual Themes,

And both, to shew his Judgment, in Extreams.

So over-violent, or over-civil,

That every Man with him was God or Devil."—*Dryden.*

Where the four verses that are accented on the last save one have eleven syllables, the others, accented on the last, but ten.

In a poem whose verses consist of eight, the double rhymes require nine; as,

"When hard Words, Jealousies, and Fears,

Set Folks together by the ears;

And made 'em fight, like mad, or drunk,

For Dame Religion as for Punk;

Whose honesty they all durst swear for,

Tho' not a Man of 'em knew wherefore:

Then did Sir Knight abandon Duelling,

And out he rode a Colonelling."—*Hudibras.*

In a poem whose verses consist of seven, the double rhymes require eight; as,

"All thy verse is softer far

Than the downy Feathers are

Of my Wings, or of my Arrows,

Of my Mother's Doves or Sparrows."—*Cowley.*

This must also be observed in blank verse; as,

"Welcome, thou worthy Partner of my Laurels!

Thou Brother of my Choice! A Band more sacred

Than Nature's brittle Tye. By holy Friendship!

Glory and Fame stood still for thy Arrival:

My Soul seem'd wanting of its better Half,

And languish'd for thy Absence like a Prophet,

Who waits the Inspiration of his God."—*Rowe.*

And this verse of Milton,

"Void of all Succour and needful Comfort,"

wants a syllable; for, being accented on the last save one, it ought to have eleven, as all the verses but two of the preceding example have. But if we transpose the words thus,

"Of Succour and all needful Comfort void,"

it then wants nothing of its due measure, because it is accented on the last syllable.

SECTION I.—*Of the several sorts of verses; and, first, of those of ten syllables: of the due observation of the accents, and of the pause.*

Our poetry admits for the most part but of three sorts of verses; that is to say, of verses of ten, eight, or seven syllables. Those of four, six, nine, eleven, twelve, and fourteen, are generally employed in masks and operas, and in the stanzas of lyric and Pindaric odes, and we have few entire poems composed in any of those sort of verses. Those of twelve and fourteen syllables are frequently inserted in our poems in heroic verse, and when rightly made use of, carry a peculiar grace with them. See the next section towards the end.

The verses of ten syllables, which are our heroic, are used in heroic poems, in tragedies, comedies, pastorals, elegies, and sometimes in burlesque.

In these verses two things are chiefly to be considered:

1. The seat of the accent.

2. The pause.

For 'tis not enough that verses have their just number of syllables; the true harmony of them depends on a due observation of the accent and pause.

The accent is an elevation or a falling of the voice on a certain syllable of a word.

The pause is a rest or stop that is made in pronouncing the verse, and that divides it, as it were, into two parts; each of which is called an hemistich, or half-verse.

But this division is not always equal, that is to say, one of the half-verses does not always contain the same number of syllables as the other. And this inequality proceeds from the seat of the accent that is strongest, and prevails most in the first half-verse. For the pause must be observed at the end of the word where such accents happen to be, or at the end of the following word.

Now, in a verse of ten syllables this accent must be either on the second, fourth, or sixth; which produces five several pauses, that is to say, at the third, fourth, fifth, sixth or seventh syllable of the verse:

For,

When it happens to be on the second, the pause will be either at the third or fourth.

At the third in two manners:

1. When the syllable accented happens to be the last save one of a word; as,

"As busy—as intentive Emmets are;

Or Cities—whom unlook'd for Sieges scare."—*Davenant.*

2. Or when the accent is on the last of a word, and the next a monosyllable, whose construction is governed by that on which the accent is; as,

"Despise it,—and more noble Thoughts pursue."—*Dryden.*

When the accent falls on the second syllable of the verse, and the last save two of a word, the pause will be at the fourth; as,

"He meditates—his absent Enemy."—*Dryden.*

When the accent is on the fourth of a verse, the pause will be either at the same syllable, or at the fifth or sixth.

At the same, when the syllable of the accent happens to be the last of a word; as,

"Such huge Extreams—inhabit thy great Mind,

God-like, unmov'd,—and yet, like Woman, kind."—*Waller.*

At the fifth in two manners:

1. When it happens to be the last save one of a word; as,

"Like bright Aurora—whose refulgent Ray

Fortells the Feavour—of ensuing Day;

And warns the Shepherd—with his Flocks, retreat

To leafy Shadows—from the threaten'd Heat."—*Waller.*

2. Or the last of the word, if the next be a monosyllable governed by it; as,

"So fresh the Wound is—and the Grief so vast."—*Waller.*

At the sixth, when the syllable of the accent happens to be the last save two of a word; as,

"Those Seeds of Luxury,—Debate, and Pride."—*Waller.*

Lastly, when the accent is on the sixth syllable of the verse, the pause will be either at the same syllable or at the seventh.

At the same, when the syllable of the accent happens to be the last of a word; as,

"She meditates Revenge—resolv'd to die."—*Waller.*

At the seventh in two manners:

1. When it happens to be the last save one of a word; as,

"Nor when the War is over,—is it Peace."—*Dryden.*

"Mirrors are taught to flatter,—but our Springs."—*Waller.*

2. Or the last of a word, if the following one be a monosyllable whose construction depends on the preceding word on which the accent is; as,

"And since he could not save her—with her dy'd."—*Dryden.*

From all this it appears, that the pause is determined by the seat of the accent; but if the accents happen to be equally strong on the second, fourth, and sixth syllable of a verse, the sense and construction of the words must then guide to the observation of the pause. For example, in one of the verses I have cited as an instance of it at the seventh syllable,

"Mirrors are taught to flatter, but our Springs."

The accent is as strong on *taught*, as on the first syllable of *flatter*; and if the pause were observed at the fourth syllable of the verse, it would have nothing disagreeable in its sound; as,

"Mirrors are taught—to flatter, but our Springs

Present th' impartial Images of things."

Which though it be no violence to the ear, yet it is to the sense, and that ought always carefully to be avoided in reading or in repeating of verses.

For this reason it is, that the construction or sense should never end at a syllable where the pause ought not to be made; as at the eighth and second in the two following verses:—

"Bright Hesper twinkles from afar:—Away

My Kids!—for you have had a Feast to Day."—*Stafford*.

Which verses have nothing disagreeable in their structure but the pause, which in the first of them must be observed at the eighth syllable, in the second at the second; and so unequal a division can produce no true harmony. And for this reason too, the pauses at the third and seventh syllables, though not wholly to be condemned, ought to be but sparingly practised.

The foregoing rules ought indispensably to be followed in all our verses of ten syllables; and the observation of them, like that of right time in music, will produce harmony; the neglect of them harshness and discord; as appears by the following verses:—

"None think Rewards render'd worthy their Worth.

And both Lovers, both thy Disciples were."

In which, though the true number of syllables be observed, yet neither of them have so much as the sound of a verse. Now their disagreeableness proceeds from the undue seat of the accent. For example, the first of them accented on the fifth and seventh syllables; but if we change the words, and remove the accent to the fourth and sixth, the verse will become smooth and easy; as,

"None think Rewards are equal to their Worth."

The harshness of the last of them proceeds from its being accented on the third syllable, which may be mended thus, by transposing only one word:

"And Lovers both, both thy Disciples were."

In like manner the following verses,

"To be massacred, not in Battle slain."—*Blac.*

"But forc'd, harsh, and uneasy unto all."—*Cowley.*

"Against the Insults of the Wind and Tide."—*Blac.*

"A second Essay will the Pow'rs appease."—*Blac.*

"With Scythians expert in the Dart and Bow."—*Dryden.*

are rough, because the foregoing rules are not observed in their structure; for example, the first where the pause is at the fifth syllable, and the accent on the third, is contrary to the rule, which says, that the accent that determines the pause must be on the second, fourth, or sixth syllable of the verse; and to mend that verse we need only place the accent on the fourth, and then the pause at the fifth will have nothing disagreeable; as,

"Thus to be murther'd, not in Battle slain."

The second verse is accented on the third syllable, and the pause is there too; which makes it indeed the thing it expresses, forced, harsh, and uneasy; it may be mended thus:

"But forc'd and harsh, uneasy unto all."

The third, fourth, and fifth of those verses have like faults; for the pauses are at the fifth, and the accent there too; which is likewise contrary to the foregoing rules. Now they will be made smooth and flowing, by taking the accent from the fifth, and removing the seat of the pause; as,

"Against th' Insults both of the Wind and Tide

A second Tryal will the Pow'rs appease.

With Scythians skilful in the Dart and Bow."

From whence we conclude, that in all verses of ten syllables, the most prevailing accents ought to be on the second, fourth, or sixth syllables; for if they are on the third, fifth, or seventh, the verses will be rough and disagreeable, as has been proved by the preceding instances.

In short, the wrong placing of the accent is as great a fault in our versification, as false quantity was in that of the ancients; and therefore we ought to take equal care to avoid it, and endeavour so to dispose the words that they may create a certain melody in the ear, without labour to the tongue, or violence to the sense.

SECTION II.—*Of the other sorts of verses that are used in our poetry.*

After the verses of ten syllables those of eight are most frequent, and we have many entire poems composed in them.

In the structure of these verses, as well as of those of ten syllables, we must take care that the most prevailing accents be neither on the third nor fifth syllables of them.

They also require a pause to be observed in pronouncing them, which is generally at the fourth or fifth syllable; as,

"I'll sing of Heroes,—and of Kings,

In mighty Numbers—mighty things;

Begin, my Muse,—but to the Strings,

To my great Song—rebellious prove,

The Strings will sound—of nought but Love."—*Cowley.*

The verses of seven syllables, which are called anacreontic, are most beautiful when the strongest accent is on the third, and the pause either there or at the fourth; as,

"Fill the Bowl—with rosy Wine,

Round our Temples—Roses twine

Crown'd with Roses—we contemn

Gyges' wealthy—Diadem."—*Cowley.*

The verses of nine and of eleven syllables, are of two sorts; one is those that are accented upon the last save one, which are only the verses of double rhyme that belong to those of eight and ten syllables, of which examples have already been given. The other of those that are accented on the last syllable, which are employed only in compositions for music, and in the lowest sort of burlesque poetry; the disagreeableness of their measure having wholly excluded them from grave and serious subjects. They who desire to see examples of them may find some scattered here and there in our masks and operas, and in the burlesque writers. I will give but two:

"Hylas, O Hylas, why sit we mute?

Now that each Bird saluteth the Spring."—*Waller.*

"Apart let me view then each Heavenly Fair,

For three at a time there's no Mortal can bear."—*Congreve.*

The verses of twelve syllables are truly heroic both in their measure and sound, though we have no entire works composed in them; and they are so far from being a blemish to the poems they are in, that on the contrary, when rightly employed, they conduce not a little to the ornament of them; particularly in the following rencontres:—

1. When they conclude an episode in an heroic poem. Thus Stafford ends his translation of that of Camilla from the eleventh Æneid with a verse of twelve syllables:

"The ling'ring Soul th' unwelcome Doom receives,

And, murm'ring with Disdain, the beauteous Body leaves."

2. When they conclude a triplet and full sense together; as,

"Millions of op'ning Mouths to Fame belong; }

And every Mouth is furnish'd with a Tongue; }

And round with list'ning Ears the flying Plague is hung." }

—*Dryden.*

And here we may observe by the way, that whenever a triplet is made use of in an heroic poem, it is a fault not to close the sense at the end of the triplet, but to continue it into the next line; as Dryden has done in his translation of the eleventh Æneid, in these lines:

"With Olives crown'd, the Presents they shall bear, }

A Purple Robe, a Royal Iv'ry Chair, }

And all the Marks of Sway that Latian Monarchs wear, }

And Sums of Gold," &c. }

And in the seventh Æneid he has committed the like fault:

"Then they, whose Mothers, frantick with their Fear, }

In Woods and Wilds the Flags of Bacchus bear, }

And lead his Dances with dishevell'd Hair, }

Increase thy Clamours," &c. }

But the sense is not confined to the couplet, for the close of it may fall into the middle of the next verse, that is, the third, and sometimes farther off, provided the last verse of the couplet exceed not the number of ten syllables; for then the sense ought always to conclude with it. Examples of this are so frequent, that it is needless to give any.

3. When they conclude the stanzas of lyric or Pindaric odes; examples of which are often seen in Dryden, and others.

In these verses the pause ought to be at the sixth syllable, as may be seen in the foregoing examples.

We sometimes find it, though very rarely, at the seventh; as,

"That such a cursed Creature—lives so long a Space."

When it is at the fourth, the verse will be rough and hobbling; as,

"And Midwife Time—the ripen'd Plot to Murther brought."

—Dryden.

"The Prince pursu'd,—and march'd along with great equal Pace."

—Dryden.

In the last of which it is very apparent, that if the sense and construction would allow us to make the pause at the sixth syllable,

"The Prince pursu'd, and march'd—along with equal pace,"

the verse would be much more flowing and easy.

The verses of fourteen syllables are less frequent than those of twelve; they are likewise inserted in heroic poems, &c., and are agreeable enough when they conclude a triplet and sense, and follow a verse of twelve; as,

"For Thee the Land in fragrant Flowers is drest; }

For thee the Ocean smiles, and smooths her wavy Breast, }

And Heav'n itself with more serene and purer Light is blest." }

—Dryden.

But if they follow one of ten syllables, the inequality of the measure renders them less agreeable; as,

"While all thy Province, Nature, I survey, }

And sing to Memmius an immortal Lay }

Of Heav'n and Earth; and everywhere thy wonderous Pow'r display." }

—Dryden.

Especially if it be the last of a couplet only; as,

"With Court-Informer's Haunts, and Royal Spies,

Things done relates, not done she feigns, and mingles Truth

with Lies."

—Dryden.

But this is only in heroics; for in their Pindarics and lyrics, verses of twelve or fourteen syllables are frequently and gracefully placed, not only after those of twelve or ten, but of any other number of syllables whatsoever.

The verses of four and six syllables have nothing worth observing, and therefore I shall content myself with having made mention of them. They are, as I said before, used only in operas and masks, and in lyric and Pindaric odes. Take one example of them:—

"To rule by love,

To shed no Blood,

May be extoll'd above;

But here below,

Let Princes know,

'Tis fatal to be good."

—Dryden.

SECTION III.—*Several rules conducing to the beauty of our versification.*

Our poetry being very much polished and refined since the days of Chaucer, Spenser, and the other ancient poets, some rules which they neglected, and that conduce very much to the ornaments of it, have been practised by the best of the moderns.

The first is to avoid as much as possible the concourse of vowels, which occasions a certain ill-sounding gaping, called by the Latins *hiatus*; and which they thought so disagreeable to the ear, that, to avoid it, whenever a word ended in a vowel, and the next began with one, they never, even in prose, sounded the vowel of the first word, but lost it in the pronunciation; and it is a fault in our poets not to do the like, whenever our language will admit of it.

For this reason the *e* of the particle the ought always to be cut off before the words that begin with a vowel; as,

"With weeping Eyes she heard th' unwelcome News."—*Dryden.*

And it is a fault to make the and the first syllable of the following word two distinct syllables, as in this,

"Restrain'd a while by the unwelcome Night."—*Waller.*

A second sort of hiatus, and that ought no less to be avoided, is when a word that ends in a vowel that cannot be cut off, is placed before one that begins with the same vowel, or one that has the like sound; as,

"Should thy Iambicks swell into a Book."—*Waller.*

The second rule is, to contract the two last syllables of the preterperfect tenses of all the verbs that will admit of it; which are all the regular verbs whatsoever, except only those ending in *d* or *t*, and *de* or *te*. And it is a fault to make amazed of three syllables, and loved of two, instead of amazed of two, and loved of one.

And the second person of the present and preterperfect tenses of all verbs ought to be contracted in like manner; as thou lov'st, for thou lovest, &c.

The third rule is, not to make use of several words in a verse that begin with the same letter; as,

"The Court he knew to Steer in Storms of State,

He in these Miracles Design discern'd."

Yet we find an instance of such a verse in Dryden's translation of the first pastoral of Virgil:

"Till then a helpless, hopeless, homely swain."

Which I am persuaded he left not thus through negligence or inadvertency, but with design to paint in the number and sound of the words the thing he described—a shepherd in whom

"Nec spes libertatis erat, nec cura peculi."

Now how far the sound of the *h* aspirate, with which three feet of that verse begin, expresses the despair of the swain, let the judicious judge. I have taken notice of it only to say, that it is a great beauty in poetry, when the words and numbers are so disposed, as by their order and sound to represent the things described.

The fourth is, to avoid ending a verse by an adjective whose substantive begins the following; as,

"Some lost their quiet Rivals, some their kind

Parents," &c.—*Davenant.*

Or, by a preposition when the case it governs begins the verse that follows; as,

"The daily less'ning of our life, shews by

A little dying, how outright to dye."

The fifth is, to avoid the frequent use of words of many syllables, which are proper enough in prose, but come not into verse without a certain violence altogether disagreeable; particularly those whose accent is on the fourth syllable from the last, as undutifulness.

SECTION IV.—*Doubts concerning the number of syllables of certain words.*

There is no language whatsoever that so often joins several vowels together to make diphthongs of them, as ours; this appears in our having several composed of three different vowels, as *eau* and *eou* in beauteous, *iou* in glorious, *uai* in acquaint, &c.

Now from hence may arise some difficulties concerning the true pronunciation of those vowels, whether they ought to be founded separately in two syllables, or jointly in one.

The ancient poets made them sometimes of two syllables, sometimes but of one, as the measure of their verse required; but they are now become to be but of one, and it is a fault to make them of two: from whence we may draw this general rule:—That whenever one syllable of a word ends in a vowel, and the next begins with one, provided the first of those syllables be not that on which the word is accented, those two syllables ought in verse to be contracted and made but one.

Thus beauteous is but two syllables, victorious but three; and it is a fault in Dryden to make it four, as he has done in this verse:

"Your arms are on the Rhine victorious."

To prove that this verse wants a syllable of its due measure, we need but add one to it; as,

"Your arms are on the Rhine victorious now."

Where, though the syllable *now* be added to the verse, it has no more than its due number of syllables; which plainly proves it wanted it.

But if the accent be upon the first of these syllables, they cannot be contracted to make a diphthong, but must be computed as two distinct syllables: thus poet, lion, quiet, and the like, must always be used as two syllables; poetry, and the like, as three. And it is a fault to make riot, for example, one syllable, as Milton has done in this verse,

"Their Riot ascends above the lofty Tow'rs."

The same poet has in another place made use of a like word twice in one verse, and made it two syllables each time;

"With Ruin upon Ruin, Rout on Rout."

And any ear may discover that this last verse has its true measure, the other not.

But there are some words that may be excepted; as diamond, violet, violent, diadem, hyacinth, and perhaps some others, which, though they are accented upon the first vowel, are sometimes used but as two syllables; as in the following verses:—

"From Diamond Quarries hewn, and Rocks of Gold."—*Milton.*

"With Poppies, Daffadils, and Violets join'd."—*Tate.*

"With vain, but violent force their Darts they flung."—*Cowley.*

"His Ephod, Mitre, well-cut Diadem on."—*Cowley.*

"My blushing Hyacinths, and my Bays I keep."—*Dryden.*

Sometimes as three; as,

"A Mount of Rocky Diamond did rise."—*Blac.*

"Hence the blue Violet and blushing Rose."—*Blac.*

"And set soft Hyacinths of Iron blue."—*Dryden.*

When they are used but as two syllables they suffer an elision of one of their vowels, and are generally written thus, di'mond, vi'let, &c.

This contraction is not always made of syllables of the same word only; for the particle *a* being placed after a word that ends in a vowel, will sometimes admit of the like contraction; for example, after the word many; as,

"Tho' many a victim from my Folds was bought,

And many a Cheese to Country Markets brought."—*Dryden.*

"They many a Trophy gain'd with many a Wound."—*Davenant.*

After *to*; as,

"Can he to a Friend, to a Son so bloody grow?"—*Cowley.*

After *they*; as,

"From thee, their long-known King, they a King desire."—*Cowley.*

After *by*; as,

"When we by a foolish Figure say."—*Cowley.*

And perhaps after some others.

There are also other words whose syllables are sometimes contracted, sometimes not; as bower, heaven, prayer, nigher, towards, and many more of the like nature, but they generally ought to be used but as one syllable; and then they suffer an elision of the vowel that precedes their final consonant, and ought to be written thus, bow'r, heav'n, pray'r, nigh'r, tow'rds.

The termination *ism* is always used but as one syllable; as,

"Where grisly Schism and raging Strife appear."—*Cowley*.

"And Rheumatisms I send to rack the Joynts."—*Dryden*.

And, indeed, considering that it has but one vowel, it may seem absurd to assert that it ought to be reckoned two syllables; yet in my opinion those verses seem to have a syllable more than their due measure, and would run better if we took one from them; as,

"Where grisly Schism, raging Strife appear,"

"I Rheumatisms send to rack the Joynts."

Yet this opinion being contrary to the constant practice of our poets, I shall not presume to advance it as a rule for others to follow, but leave it to be decided by such as are better judges of poetical numbers.

The like may be said of the terminations *asm* and *osm*.

SECTION V.—*Of the elisions that are allowed in our versification.*

In verses consisting only of a certain number of syllables, nothing can be of more ease, or greater use to poets, than the retaining or cutting off a syllable from a verse, according as the measure of it requires; and therefore it is requisite to treat of the elisions that are allowable in our poetry, some of which have been already taken notice of in the preceding section.

By elision I mean the cutting off one or more letters from a word, whereby two syllables come to be contracted into one, or the taking away an entire syllable. Now when in a word of more than two syllables, which is accented on the last save two, the liquid *r* happens to be between two vowels, that which precedes the liquid admits of an elision. Of this nature are many words in *ance*, *ence*, *ent*, *er*, *ous*, and *ry*; as temperance, preference, different, flatterer, amorous, victory: which are words of three syllables, and often used as such in verse; but they may be also contracted into two by cutting off the vowel that precedes the liquid, as temp'rance, pref'rence, diff'rent, flatt'rer, am'rous, vict'ry. The like elision is sometimes used when any of the other liquids *l*, *m*, or *n*, happen to be between two vowels in words accented like the former; as fabulous, enemy, mariner, which may be contracted fab'lous, en'my, mar'ner. But this is not so frequent.

Observe, that I said accented on the last save two; for if the word be accented on the last save one, that is to say, on the vowel that precedes the liquid, that vowel may not be cut off. And therefore it is a fault to make, for example, sonorous two syllables, as in this verse;

"With Son'rous Metals wak'd the drowsy Day."—*Blac.*

Which always ought to be three, as in this,

"Sonorous Metals blowing martial sounds."—*Milton.*

In like manner, whenever the letter *s* happens to be between two vowels in words of three syllables, accented on the first, one of the vowels may be cut off; as pris'ner, bus'ness, &c.

Or the letter *c* when it is sounded like *s*; that is to say, whenever it precedes the vowel *e* or *i*; as med'cine for medicine. Or *v* consonant, as cov'nant for covenant.

To these may be added the gerunds of all verbs whose infinities end in any of the liquids, preceded by a vowel or a diphthong, and that are accented on the last save one; for the gerunds being formed by adding the syllable *ing* to the infinitive, the liquid that was their final letter comes thereby to be between two vowels; and the accent that was on the last save one of the infinitive, comes to be on the last save two of the gerunds: and therefore the vowel or diphthong that precedes the liquid may be cut off; by means whereof the gerund of three syllables comes to be but of two; as from travel, travelling, or trav'ling; from endeavour, endeavouring, or endeav'ring, &c.

But if the accent be on the last syllable of such a verb, its gerund will not suffer such an elision. Thus the gerund of devour must always be three syllables, devouring, not dev'ring; because all derivatives still retain the accent of their primitives, that is, on the same syllable; and the accent always obliges the syllable on which it is to remain entire.

The gerunds of the verbs in *ow*, accented on the last save two, suffer an elision of the *o* that precedes the *w*; as foll'wing, wall'wing.

The particle *it* admits of an elision of its vowel before it was, were, will, would; as 'tis, 'twas, 'twere, 'twill, 'twould, for it is, it was, &c.

It likewise sometimes suffers the like elision when placed after a word that ends in a vowel; as by't for by it, do't for do it; or that ends in a consonant after which the letter *t* can be pronounced; as was't for was it, in't for in it, and the like. But this is not so frequent in heroic verse.

The particle *is* may lose its *i* after any word that ends in a vowel, or in any of the consonants after which the letter *s* may be sounded; as she's for she is, the air's for the air is, &c.

To (sign of the infinitive mood) may lose its *o* before any verb that begins with a vowel; as t'maze, t'undo, &c.

To (sign of the dative case) may likewise lose its *o* before any noun that begins with a vowel; as t'air, t'every, &c. But this elision is not so allowable as the former.

Are may lose its *a* after the pronouns personal, we, you, they; as we're, you're, they're. And thus it is that this elision ought to be made, and not, as some do, by cutting off the final vowels of the pronouns personal, w'are, y'are, th'are.

Will and would may lose all their first letters, and retain only their final one, after any of the pronouns personal; as I'll for I will, he'd for he would; or after who, who'll for who will, who'd for who would.

Have may lose its two first letters after I, you, we, they; as I've, you've, we've, they've.

Not, its two first letters after can; as can't for cannot.

Am, its *a* after *i*; I'm for I am.

Us, its *u* after let; let's for let us.

Taken, its *k*, ta'en; for so it ought to be written, not ta'ne.

Heaven, seven, even, eleven, and the participles driven, given, thriven, and their compounds, may lose their last vowel; as heav'n, forgiv'n, &c. See the foregoing section.

To these may be added, bow'r, pow'r, flow'r, tow'r, show'r, for bower, tower, &c.

Never, ever, over, may lose their *v*, and are contracted thus, ne'er, e'er, o'er.

Some words admit of an elision of their first syllable; as 'tween, 'twixt, 'mong, 'mongst, 'gainst, 'bove, 'cause, 'fore, for between, betwixt, among, amongst, against, above, because, before, and some others that may be observed in reading our poets.

I have already, in the third section of this chapter, spoken of the elision of the *e* of the particle the before vowels; but it is requisite likewise to take notice, that it sometimes loses its vowel before a word that begins with a consonant, and then its two remaining letters are joined to the preceding word; as to th' wall for to the wall, by th' wall for by the wall, &c., but this is scarcely allowable in heroic poetry.

The particles in, of, and on, sometimes lose their consonants, and are joined to the particle the in like manner, as i'th', o'th', for in the, of the.

In some of our poets we find the pronoun his loses its two first letters after any word that ends in a vowel; as to's, by's, &c., for to his, by his, &c.; or after many words that end in a consonant, after which the letter *s* can be pronounced; as in's, for's, for in his, for his, &c. This is frequent in Cowley, who often takes too great liberty in his contractions; as t'your for to your, t'which for to which, and many others; in which we must be cautious in following his example, but the contracting of the pronoun his in the manner I mentioned is not wholly to be condemned.

We sometimes find the word who contracted before words that begin with a vowel; as,

"Wh' expose to Scorn and Hate both them and it."—*Cowley*.

And the preposition in like manner; as,

"B' unequal Fate and Providence's Crime."—*Dryden*.
"Well did he know how Palms b' Oppression speed."—*Cowley*.

And the pronouns personal, he, she, they, we; as,

"Timely h' obeys her wise Advice, and strait
To unjust Force sh' opposes just Deceit."—*Cowley*.

"Themselves at first against themselves th' excite."—*Cowley*.

"Shame and Woe to us, if w' our Wealth obey."—*Cowley*.

But these and the like contractions are very rare in our most correct poets, and indeed ought wholly to be avoided, for 'tis a general rule that no vowel can be cut off before another, when it cannot be sunk in the pronunciation of it: and therefore we ought to take care never to place a word that begins with a vowel after a word that ends in one (mute *e* only excepted), unless the final vowel of the former can be lost in its pronunciation, for to leave two vowels opening on each other, causes a very disagreeable hiatus. Whenever therefore a vowel ends a word, the next ought to begin with a consonant, or what is equivalent to it; as our *w* and *h* aspirate plainly are.

For which reason it is a fault in some of our poets to cut off the *e* of the particle the; for example, before a word that begins by an *h* aspirate; as,

"And th' hasty Troops march'd loud and cheerful down."—*Cowley*.

But if the *h* aspirate be followed by another *e*, that of the particle the may be cut off; as,

"Th' Heroick Prince's Courage or his love."—*Waller*.

Th' Hesperian Fruit, and made the Dragon sleep."—*Waller*.

CHAPTER II.

OF RHYME.

SECTION I.—*What rhyme is, and the several sorts of it.*

Rhyme is a likeness or uniformity of sound in the terminations of two words. I say of sound, not of letters; for the office of rhyme being to content and please the ear, and not the eye, the sound only is to be regarded, not the writing: thus maid and persuade, laugh and quaff, though they differ in writing, rhyme very well: but plough and cough, though their terminations are written alike, rhyme not at all.

In our versification we may observe three several sorts of rhyme: single, double, and treble.

The single rhyme is of two sorts: one, of the words that are accented on the last syllable; another, of those that have their accent on the last save two.

The words accented on the last syllable, if they end in a consonant, or mute *e*, oblige the rhyme to begin at the vowel that precedes their last consonant, and to continue to the end of the word. In a consonant; as,

"Here might be seen, the Beauty, Wealth, and Wit,

And Prowess, to the Pow'r of Love submit."

—Dryden.

In mute *e*; as,

"A Spark of Virtue, by the deepest Shade

Of sad Adversity, is fairer made."

—Waller.

But if a diphthong precede the last consonant the rhyme must begin at that vowel of it whose sound most prevails; as,

"Next to the Pow'r of making Tempest cease,

Was in that storm to have so calm a Peace."

—Waller.

If the words accented on the last syllable end in any of the vowels, except mute *e*, or in a diphthong, the rhyme is made only to that vowel or diphthong. To the vowel; as,

"So wing'd with Praise we penetrate the Sky,

Teach Clouds and Stars to praise him as we fly."—*Waller.*

To the diphthong; as,

"So hungry Wolves, tho' greedy of their Prey,

Stop when they find a Lion in the Way."—*Waller.*

The other sort of single rhyme is of the words that have their accent on the last syllable save two, and these rhyme to the other in the same manner as the former; that is to say, if they end in any of the vowels, except mute *e*, the rhyme is made only to that vowel; as,

"So seems to speak the youthful Deity;

Voice, Colour, Hair, and all like Mercury."—*Waller.*

But if they end in a consonant or mute *e*, the rhyme must begin at the vowel that precedes that consonant, and continue to the end of the word; as has been shewn by the former examples.

But we must take notice, that all the words that are accented on the last save two, will rhyme not only to one another, but also to all the words whose terminations have the same sound, though they are accented on the last syllable. Thus tenderness rhymes not only to poetess, wretchedness, and the like, that are accented on the last save two, but also to confess, excess, &c., that are accented on the last; as,

"Thou art my Father now these Words confess That Name, and that indulgent Tenderness."—*Dryden.*

SECTION II.—*Of double and treble rhyme.*

All words that are accented on the last save one, require rhyme to begin at the vowel of that syllable, and to continue to the end of the word; and this is what we call double rhyme; as,

"Then all for Women, Painting, Rhyming, Drinking,

Besides ten thousands Freaks that dy'd in Thinking."—*Dryden.*

But it is convenient to take notice, that the ancient poets did not always observe this rule, and took care only that the last syllables of the words should be alike in sound without any regard to the seat of the accent. Thus nation and affection, tenderness and hapless, villany and gentry, follow and willow, and the like, were allowed as rhymes to each other in the days of Chaucer, Spenser, and the rest of the ancients; but this is now become a fault in our versification; and these two verses of Cowley rhyme not at all,

"A dear and lively Brown was Merab's Dye;

Such as the proudest Colours might envy."

Nor these of Dryden,

"Thus Air was void of Light, and Earth unstable,

And Waters dark Abyss unnavigable."

Because we may not place an accent on the last syllable of envy, nor on the last save one of unnavigable; which nevertheless we must be obliged to do, if we make the first of them rhyme to dye, the last to unstable.

But we may observe, that in burlesque poetry it is permitted to place an accent upon a syllable that naturally has none; as,

"When Pulpit, Drum Ecclesiastick,

Was beat with Fist instead of a Stick."

Where, unless we pronounce the particle *a* with a strong accent upon it, and make it sound like the vowel *a* in the last syllable but one of ecclesiastic, the verse will lose all its beauty and rhyme. But this is allowable in burlesque poetry only.

Observe that these double rhymes may be composed of two several words, provided the accent be on the last syllable of the first of them; as these verses of Cowley, speaking of gold,

"A Curse on him who did refine it,

A Curse on him who first did coin it."

Or some of the verses may end in an entire word, and the rhyme to it be composed of several; as,

"Tho' stor'd with Deletery Med'cines

Which whosoever took is dead since."—*Hudibras.*

The treble rhyme is very seldom used, and ought wholly to be exploded from serious subjects; for it has a certain flatness unworthy the gravity required in heroic verse. In which Dryden was of opinion, that even the double rhymes ought very cautiously to find place; and in all his translations of Virgil he has made use of none, except only in such words as admit of a contraction, and therefore cannot properly be said to be double rhymes; as giv'n, driv'n, tow'r, pow'r, and the like. And indeed, considering their measure is indifferent from that of a heroic verse, which consists but of ten syllables, they ought not to be too frequently used in heroic poems; but they are very graceful in the lyric, to which, as well as to the burlesque, those rhymes more properly belong.

SECTION III.—*Further instructions concerning rhyme.*

The consonants that precede the vowels where the rhyme begins, must be different in sound, and not the same; for then the rhyme will be too perfect; as light, delight; vice, advice, and the like; for though such rhymes were allowable in the days of Spenser and the other old poets, they are not so now, nor can there be any music in one single note. Cowley himself owns, that they ought not to be allowed except in Pindaric odes, which is a sort of free poetry, and there too very sparingly and not without a third rhyme to answer to both; as,

"In barren Age wild and inglorious lye,

And boast of past Fertility,

The poor relief of present Poverty."—*Cowley.*

Where the words fertility and poverty rhyme very well to the last word of the first verse, lye; but cannot rhyme to each other, because the consonants that precede the last vowels are the same, both in writing and sound.

But this is yet less allowable, if the accent be on the last syllable of the rhyme; as,

"Her Language melts Omnipotence, arrests

His hand, and thence the vengeful Light'ning wrests."—*Blac.*

From hence it follows, that a word cannot rhyme to itself though the signification be different; as, he leaves to the leaves, &c.

Nor the words that differ both in writing and sense, if they have the same sound, as maid and made, prey and pray, to bow and a bough; as,

"How gaudy Fate may be in Presents sent,

And creep insensible by Touch or Scent."—*Oldham.*

Nor a compound to its simple; as move to remove, taught to untaught, &c.

Nor the compounds of the same words to one another, as disprove to approve, and the like. All which proceeds from what I said before, viz., that the consonants that precede the vowels where the rhyme begins, must not be the same in sound, but different. In all which we vary from our neighbours; for neither the French, Italians, nor Spaniards, will allow, that a rhyme can be too perfect; and we meet with frequent examples in their poetry, where not only the compounds rhyme to their simples, and to themselves, but even where words written and pronounced exactly alike, provided they have a different signification, are made use of as rhymes to another. But this is not permitted in our poetry.

We must take care not to place a word at the middle of a verse that rhymes to the last word of it; as,

"So young in show, as if he still should grow."

But this fault is still more inexcusable, if the second verse rhyme to the middle and end of the first; as,

"Knowledge he only sought, and so soon caught,

As if for him Knowledge had rather sought."—*Cowley.*

"Here Passion sways, but there the Muse shall raise

Eternal Monuments of louder Praise."—*Waller.*

Or both the middle and end of the second to the last word of the first; as,

"Farewell, she cry'd, my Sister, thou dear Part,

Thou sweetest Part of my divided Heart."—*Dryden.*

Where the tenderness of expression will not atone for the jingle.

CHAPTER III.

OF THE SEVERAL SORTS OF POEMS, OR COMPOSITION IN
VERSE.

All our poems may be divided into two sorts: the first are those composed in couplets; the second those that are composed in stanzas, consisting of several verses.

SECTION I.—*Of the poems composed in couplets.*

In the poems composed in couplets, the rhymes follow one another, and end at each couplet; that is to say, the second verse rhymes to the first, the fourth to the third, the sixth to the fifth, and in like manner to the end of the poem.

The verses employed in this sort of poems are either verses of ten syllables; as,

> "Oh! could I flow like thee, and make thy Stream
>
> My great Example, as it is my Theme;
>
> Tho' dark yet clear; tho' gentle, yet not dull;
>
> Strong without Rage; without o'erflowing full."—*Denham.*

Or of eight; as,

> "O fairest Piece of well-form'd Earth,
>
> Why urge you thus your haughty Birth?
>
> The Pow'r, which you have o'er us lies,
>
> Not in your Race, but in your Eyes.
>
> Smile but on me, and you shall scorn
>
> Henceforth to be of Princes born:
>
> I can describe the shady Grove,
>
> Where your lov'd Mother slept with Jove:
>
> And yet excuse the faultless Dame,
>
> Caught with her Spouse's Shape and Name:
>
> Thy matchless Form will credit bring,
>
> To all the Wonders I shall sing."—*Waller.*

Or of seven; as,

> "Phillis, why should we delay
>
> Pleasures shorter than the Day?
>
> Could we, which we never can,
>
> Stretch our Lives beyond their Span,

Beauty like a Shadow flies,

And our Youth before us dies.

Or would Youth and Beauty stay,

Love has Wings, and will away.

Love has swifter Wings than Time."

But the second verse of the couplet does not always contain a like number of syllables with the first; as,

"What shall I do to be for ever known,

And make the Age to come my own?

I shall like Beast and common People die,

Unless you write my Elegy."

In the poems composed of stanzas, each stanza contains a certain number of verses, consisting for the most part of a different number of syllables; and a poem that consists of several stanzas we generally call an ode; and this is lyric poetry.

But we must not forget to observe, that our ancient poets frequently made use of intermixed rhyme in their heroic poems, which they disposed into stanzas and cantos. Thus the "Troilus and Cressida" of Chaucer is composed in stanzas consisting of seven verses; the "Fairy Queen" of Spenser in stanzas of nine, &c.; and this they took from the Italians, whose heroic poems generally consist in stanzas of eight. But this is now wholly laid aside, and Davenant, who composed his "Gondibert" in stanzas of four verses in alternate rhyme, was the last that followed their example of intermingling rhymes in heroic poetry.

The stanzas employed in our poetry cannot consist of less than three, and are seldom of more than twelve verses, except in Pindaric odes, where the stanzas are different from one another in number of verses, as shall be shown.

But to treat of all the different stanzas that are employed or may be admitted in our poetry would be a labour no less tedious than useless; it being easy to demonstrate that they may be varied almost to an infinity, that would be different from one another, either in the number of the verses of each stanza, or in the number of the syllables of each verse; or, lastly, in the various intermingling of the rhyme. I shall therefore confine myself to mention only such as are most frequently used by the best of our modern poets. And first of the stanzas consisting of three verses.

In the stanzas of three verses, or triplets, the verses of each stanza rhyme to one another, and are either heroic; as,

"Nothing, thou elder Brother even to Shade! }

Thou hadst a Being ere the World was made, }

And (well fix'd) art alone of ending not afraid."—*Rochester.* }

Or else they consist of eight syllables; as these of Waller, "Of a fair lady playing with a snake,"

"Strange that such Horror and such Grace }

Should dwell together in one Place, }

A Fairy's Arm, an Angel's Face." }

Nor do the verses of the stanzas always contain a like number of syllables; for the first and third may have ten, the second but eight; as,

"Men without Love have oft so cunning grown, }

That something like it they have shown, }

But none who had it, ever seem'd t'have none." }

"Love's of a strangely open, simple Kind, }

Can no Arts or Disguises find; }

But thinks none sees it, 'cause itself is blind."—*Cowley.* }

In the stanzas of four verses, the rhyme may be intermixed in two different manners; for either the first and third verse may rhyme to each other, and by consequence the second and fourth, and this is called alternate rhyme; or the first and fourth may rhyme, and by consequence the second and third.

But there are some poems, in stanzas of four verses, where the rhymes follow one another, and the verses differ in number of syllables only; as in Cowley's "Hymn to the Light," which begins thus—

"First-born of Chaos! who so fair didst come

From the old Negro's darksome Womb:

Which, when it saw the lovely Child,

The melancholy Mass put on kind Looks and smil'd."

But these stanzas are generally in alternate rhyme, and the verses either consist of ten syllables; as,

"She ne'er saw Courts, but Courts could have undone

With untaught Looks and an unpractis'd Heart:

Her nets the most prepar'd could never shun;

For Nature spread them in the scorn of Art."—*Davenant.*

Or of eight; as,

"Had Echo with so sweet a Grace,

Narcissus loud Complaint return'd:

Not for Reflection of his Face,

But of his Voice the Boy had burn'd."—*Waller.*

Or of ten and eight, that is to say, the first and third of ten, the second and fourth of eight; as,

"Love from Time's Wings has stol'n the Feathers sure

He has, and put them to his own:

For Hours of late as long as Days endure,

And very Minutes Hours are grown."—*Cowley.*

Or of eight and six in the like manner; as,

"Then ask not Bodies doom'd to die,

To what Abode they go:

Since Knowledge is but Sorrow's Spy,

'Tis better not to know."—*Davenant.*

Or of seven; as,

"Not the silver Doves that fly,

Yoak'd in Cythera's Car;

Nor the Wings that lift so high,

And convey her Son so far,

Are so lovely sweet and fair,

Or do more ennoble Love;

Are so choicely match'd a Pair,

Or with more consent do move."—*Waller.*

Note.—That it is absolutely necessary that both the construction and sense should end with the stanza, and not fall into the beginning of the following one as it does in the last example, which is a fault wholly to be avoided.

The stanzas of six verses are generally only one of the before-mentioned quadrans or stanzas of four verses, with two verses at the end, that rhyme to one another; as,

"A rural Judge dispos'd of Beauty's Prize,

A simple Shepherd was preferr'd to Jove:

Down to the Mountains from the Partial Skies,

Came Juno, Pallas, and, the Queen of Love,

To plead for that which was so justly giv'n,

To the bright Carlisle of the Courts of Heaven."

Where the four first verses are only a quadran, and consist of ten syllables, each in alternate rhyme.

The following stanza, in like manner, is composed of a quadran, whose verses consist of eight syllables, and to which two verses that rhyme to one another are added to the end; as,

"Hope waits upon the flow'ry Prime,

And Summer, tho' it be less gay,

Yet is not look'd on as a Time

Of Declination and Decay;

For with a full Hand that does bring

All that was promis'd by the Spring."—*Waller.*

Sometimes the quadran ends the stanza, and the two lines of the same rhyme begin it; as,

"Here's to thee, Dick; this whining Love despise;

Pledge me my Friend, and drink till thou be'st wise.

It sparkles brighter far than she;

'Tis pure and right without Deceit;

And such no Woman e'er can be:

No; they are all sophisticate."—*Cowley.*

Or as in these, where the first and last verse of the stanza consist of ten syllables,

"When Chance or cruel Bus'ness parts us two,

What do our Souls, I wonder, do?

While Sleep does our dull Bodies tie,

Methinks at Home they should not stay,

Content with Dreams, but boldly fly

Abroad, and meet each other half the way."—*Cowley.*

Or as in the following stanza, where the fourth and fifth verses rhyme to each other, and the third and sixth,

"While what I write I do not see,

I dare thus ev'n to you write Poetry.

Ah! foolish Muse! thou dost so high aspire,

And knows't her judgment well,

How much it does thy Pow'r excel;

Yet dar'st be read by thy just Doom the Fire."—*Cowley.*

(Written in Juice of Lemon.)

But in some of these stanzas the rhymes follow one another; as,

"Take heed, take heed, thou lovely Maid,

Nor be by glitt'ring Ills betray'd:

Thyself for Money! Oh! let no Man know

The Price of Beauty fall'n so low.

What Dangers ought'st thou not to dread,

When Love, that's blind, is by blind Fortune led?"—*Cowley.*

Lastly, some of these stanzas are composed of two triplets; as,

"The Lightning which tall Oaks oppose in vain,

To strike sometimes does not disdain

The humble Furzes of the Plain.

She being so high and I so low,

Her Pow'r by this does greater show,

Who at such Distance gives so sure a blow."—*Cowley.*

I have already said that the Italians compose their heroic poems in stanzas of eight verses, where the rhyme is disposed as follows: The first, third, and fifth verses rhyme to one another, and the second, fourth, and sixth, the two last always rhyme to each other. Now our translators of their heroic poems have observed the same stanza and disposition of rhyme, of which take the following example from Fairfax's translation of Tasso's "Goffredo," cant. 1, stan. 3,

"Thither thou know'st the World is best inclin'd,

Where luring Parnass most his Beams imparts;

And Truth, convey'd in verse of gentlest Kind,

To read sometimes will move the dullest Hearts;

So we, if Children young diseas'd we find,

Anoint with Sweets the Vessel's foremost parts,

To make them take the Potions sharp we give;

They drink deceiv'd, and so deceiv'd they live."

But our poets seldom employ this stanza in compositions of their own; where the following stanza of eight verses are most frequent,

"Some others may with Safety tell

The mod'rate Flames which in them dwell;

And either find some Med'cine there,

Or cure themselves ev'n by Despair:

My Love's so great, that it might prove

Dang'rous to tell her that I love.

So tender is my Wound it cannot bear

Any Salute, tho' of the kindest Air."—*Cowley*.

Where the rhymes follow one another, and the six first verses consist of eight syllables each, the two last of ten.

We have another sort of stanza of eight verses, where the fourth rhymes to the first, the third to the second, and the four last are two couplets; and where the first, fourth, sixth, and eighth are of ten syllables each, the four others but of eight; as,

"I've often wish'd to love: What shall I do?

Me still the cruel Boy does spare;

And I a double Task must bear,

First to woo him, and then a Mistress too.

Come at last, and strike for shame,

If thou art any Thing besides a Name;

I'll think thee else no God to be,

But Poets rather Gods, who first created thee."—*Cowley.*

Another, when the two first and two last verses consist of ten syllables each, and rhyme to one another, the four other but of eight in alternate rhyme.

"Tho' you be absent hence, I needs must say,

The Trees as beauteous are, and Flow'rs as gay,

As ever they were wont to be:

Nay the Birds rural Musick too

Is as melodious and free,

As if they sung to pleasure you.

I saw a Rose bud ope this Morn; I'll swear

The blushing Morning open'd not more fair."—*Cowley.*

Another, where the four first verses are two couplets, the four last in alternate rhyme; as in Cowley's "Ode of a Lady that made Posies for Rings,"

"I little thought the Time would ever be,

That I should Wit in dwarfish Posies see,

As all Words in few Letters live,

Thou to few Words all Sense dost give.

'Twas Nature taught you this rare Art,

In such a Little, Much to show;

Who all the Good she did impart

To womankind, epitomiz'd in you.

SECTION V.—*Of the stanzas of ten and twelve verses.*

The stanzas of ten and twelve verses are seldom employed in our poetry, it being very difficult to confine ourselves to a certain disposition of rhyme, and measure of verse, for so many lines together; for which reason those of four, six, and eight verses are the most frequent. However, we sometimes find some of ten and twelve; as in Cowley's ode, which he calls "Verses Lost upon a Wager," where the rhymes follow one another; but the verses differ in the number of syllables.

"As soon hereafter will I Wagers lay

'Gainst what an Oracle shall say;

Fool that I was to venture to deny

A Tongue so us'd to Victory;

A Tongue so blest by Nature and by Art,

That never yet it spoke, but gain'd a heart.

Tho' what you said had not been true,

If spoke by any else but you;

Your speech will govern Destiny,

And Fate will change rather than you shall lye."—*Cowley.*

The same poet furnishes us with an example of a stanza of twelve verses in the ode he calls "The Prophet," where the rhymes are observed in the same manner as in the former examples.

"Teach me to love! Go teach thy self Wit:

I chief Professor am of it.

Teach Craft to Scots, and Thrift to Jews,

Teach Boldness to the Stews.

In Tyrants Courts teach supple Flattery,

Teach Jesuits that have travell'd far too lie,

Teach fire to burn, and Winds to blow,

Teach restless Fountains how to flow,

Teach the dull Earth fixt to abide,

Teach Womankind Inconstancy and Pride,

See if your Diligence there will useful prove;
But prithee teach not me to love."

SECTION VI.—*Of the stanzas that consist of an odd*

number of verses.

We have also stanzas that consist of odd numbers of verses, as of five, seven, nine, and eleven; in all which it of necessity follows that three verses of the stanza rhyme to one another, or that one of them be a blank verse.

In the stanzas of five verses the first and third may rhyme, and the second and two last; as,

"See not my Love how Time resumes

The Beauty which he lent these Flow'rs:

Tho' none should taste of their Perfumes,

Yet they must live but some few Hours:

Time what we forbear devours."—*Waller.*

Which is only a stanza of four verses in alternate rhyme, to which a fifth verse is added that rhymes to the second and fourth.

See also an instance of a stanza of five verses, where the rhymes are intermixed in the manner as the former, but the first and third verses are composed but of four syllables each.

"Go, lovely Rose,

Tell her that wastes her time and me,

That now she knows,

When I resemble her to thee,

How sweet and fair she seems to be."—*Waller.*

In the following example the two first verses rhyme, and the three last.

"'Tis well, 'tis well with them, said I,

Whose short-liv'd Passions with themselves can die.

For none can be unhappy, who }

'Midst all his Ills a Time does know, }

Tho' ne'er so long, when he shall not be so."—*Cowley.* }

In this stanza the two first and the last, and the third and fourth rhyme to one another.

"It is enough, enough of Time and Pain

Hast thou consum'd in vain;

Leave, wretched Cowley, leave,

Thy self with Shadows to deceive.

Think that already lost which thou must never gain."—*Cowley*.

The stanzas of seven verses are frequent enough in our poetry, especially among the ancients, who composed many of their poems in this sort of stanza; see the example of one of them taken from Spenser in the "Ruins of Time," where the first and third verses rhyme to one another, the second, fourth, and fifth, and the two last.

"But Fame with golden Wings aloft does fly

Above the Reach of ruinous Decay,

And with brave Plumes does beat the Azure Sky,

Admir'd of base-born Men from far away:

Then whoso will with virtuous Deeds assay,

To mount to Heaven, on Pegasus must ride,

And in sweet Poets verse be glorify'd."

I have rather chosen to take notice of this stanza, because that poet and Chaucer have made use of it in many of their poems, though they have not been followed in it by any of the moderns, whose stanzas of seven verses are generally composed as follows.

Either the four first verses are a quadran in alternate rhyme, and the three last rhyme to one another; as,

"Now by my Love, the greatest Oath that is,

None loves you half so well as I;

I do not ask your Love for this;

But for Heav'ns sake believe me or I die.

No Servant sure but did deserve }

His Master should believe that he did serve; }

And I'll ask no more Wages, tho' I starve." }

Or the four first two couplets, and the three last a triplet; as,

"Indeed I must confess

When Souls mix 'tis a Happiness,

But not compleat 'till Bodies too combine,

And closely as our Minds together join.

But half of Heav'n the Souls in Glory taste }

'Till by Love in Heav'n at last }

Their Bodies too are plac'd." }

Or, on the contrary, the three first may rhyme, and the four last be in rhymes that follow one another; as,

"From Hate, Fear, Hope, Anger, and Envy free, }

And all the Passions else that be, }

In vain I boast of Liberty: }

In vain this State a Freedom call,

Since I have Love; and Love is all.

Sot that I am! who think it fit to brag

That I have no Disease besides the Plague."—*Cowley*.

Or the first may rhyme to the two last, the second to the fifth, and third and fourth to one another; as,

"In vain thou drowsy God I thee invoke,

For thou who dost from Fumes arise,

Thou who Man's Soul dost overshade

With a thick Cloud by Vapours made,

Canst have no Pow'r to shut his Eyes,

Or Passage of his Spirits to choak,

Whose Flame's so pure, that it sends up no Smoak."—*Cowley*.

Or lastly, the four first and two last may be in the following rhyme, and the fifth a blank verse; as,

"Thou robb'st my Days of Bus'ness and Delights,

Of Sleep thou robb'st my Nights.

Ah lovely Thief! what wilt thou do?

What, rob me of Heav'n too!

Thou e'en my Prayers dost from me steal,

And I with wild Idolatry

Begin to God, and end them all in thee."—*Cowley.*

The stanzas of nine and of eleven syllables are not so frequent as those of five and seven. Spenser has composed his "Fairy Queen" in stanzas of nine verses, where the first rhymes to the third, the second to the fourth, fifth and seventh, and the sixth to the last; but this stanza is very difficult to maintain, and the unlucky choice of it reduced him often to the necessity of making use of many exploded words; nor has he, I think, been followed in it by any of the moderns, whose six first verses of the stanzas that consist of nine are generally in rhymes that follow one another, and the three last a triplet; as,

"Beauty, Love's Scene and Masquerade,

So well by well-plac'd Lights, and Distance made;

False Coin! with which th' Imposter cheats us still,

The Stamp and Colour good, but Metal ill:

Which light or base we find, when we

Weigh by Enjoyment, and examine thee.

For tho' thy Being be but Show,

'Tis chiefly Night which Men to thee allow,

And chuse t' enjoy thee, when thou least art thou."

—*Cowley.*

In the following example the like rhyme is to be observed, but the verses differ in measure from the former,

"Beneath this gloomy Shade,

By Nature only for my Sorrows made,

I'll spend this Voice in Cries;

In Tears I'll waste these Eyes,

By Love so vainly fed;

So Lust of old the Deluge punished.

Ah wretched Youth! said I;

Ah wretched Youth! twice did I sadly cry;

Ah wretched Youth! the Fields and Floods reply."—*Cowley.*

The stanzas consisting of eleven verses are yet less frequent than those of nine, and have nothing particular to be observed in them. Take an example of one of them, where the six first are three couplets, the three next a triplet, the two last a couplet; and where the fourth, the seventh, and the last verses are of ten syllables each, the others of eight,

"No, to what Purpose should I speak?

No, wretched Heart, swell till you break:

She cannot love me if she would,

And, to say Truth, 'twere Pity that she should.

No, to the Grave thy Sorrows bear,

As silent as they will be there;

Since that lov'd Hand this mortal Wound does give.

So handsomely the Thing contrive,

That she may guiltless of it live:

So perish, that her killing thee

May a Chance-Medley, and no Murder be."—*Cowley.*

SECTION VII.—*Of Pindaric odes, and poems in blank verse.*

The stanzas of Pindaric odes are neither confined to a certain number of verses, nor the verses to a certain number of syllables, nor the rhymes to a certain distance. Some stanzas contain fifty verses or more, others not above ten, and sometimes not so many; some verses fourteen, nay, sixteen syllables, others not above four: sometimes the rhymes follow one another for several couplets together, sometimes they are removed six verses from each other; and all this in the same stanza. Cowley was the first who introduced this sort of poetry into our language: nor can the nature of it be better described than as he himself has done it, in one of the stanzas of his ode upon liberty, which I will transcribe, not as an example, for none can properly be given where no rule can be prescribed; but to give an idea of the nature of this sort of poetry.

"If Life should a well-order'd Poem be,

In which he only hits the White,

Who joins true Profit with the best Delight;

The more heroick Strain let others take,

Mine the Pindarick Way I'll make:

The Matter shall be grave, the Numbers loose and free;

It shall not keep one settled Pace to Time,

In the same Tune it shall not always Chime,

Nor shall each Day just to his Neighbour rhyme.

A thousand Liberties it shall dispense,

And yet shall manage all without Offence,

Or to the Sweetness of the Sound, or Greatness of the Sense,

Nor shall it ever from one Subject start,

Nor seek Transitions to depart;

Nor its set Way o'er Stiles and Bridges make,

Nor thro' Lanes a compass take,

As if fear'd some Trespass to commit,

When the wide Air's a Road for it.

So the Imperial Eagle does not stay

'Till the whole Carcass he devour,

That's fall'n into his Pow'r,

As if his gen'rous Hunger understood,

That he can never want Plenty of Food;

He only sucks the tasteful Blood,

And to fresh Game flies cheerfully away,

To Kites and meaner Birds, he leaves the mangled Prey."

This sort of poetry is employed in all manner of subjects; in pleasant, in grave, in amorous, in heroic, in philosophical, in moral, and in divine.

Blank verse is where the measure is exactly kept without rhyme. Shakespeare, to avoid the troublesome constraint of rhyme, was the first who invented it; our poets since him have made use of it in many of their tragedies and comedies; but the most celebrated poem in this kind of verse is Milton's "Paradise Lost," from the fifth book of which I have taken the following lines for an example of blank verse.

"These are thy glorious Works, Parent of Good!

Almighty! thine this universal Frame,

Thus wond'rous fair! thyself how wond'rous then!

Speak you, who best can tell, ye Sons of Light,

Angels! for you behold him, and with Songs,

And Choral Symphonies, Day without Night,

Circle his Throne rejoycing, you in Heaven.

On Earth, join all ye Creatures, to extol

Him first, him last, him midst, and without End!

Fairest of Stars, last in the Train of Night,

If better thou belong not to the Dawn,

Sure Pledge of Day, that crown'st the smiling Morn

With the bright Circlet, praise him in thy Sphere,

While Day arises, that sweet hour of Prime!

Thou Sun! of this great World both Eye and Soul,

Acknowledge him thy Creator, sound his Praise

In thy eternal Course, both when thou climb'st,

And when high Noon hast gain'd and when thou fall'st.

Moon! that now meet'st the Orient Sun, now fly'st

With the fix'd Stars, fix'd in their Orb that flies,

And ye five other wand'ring Fires! that move

In Mystick Dance, not without Song resound

His Praise, who out of Darkness call'd up Light.

Air! and ye Element! the eldest Birth

Of Nature's Womb, that in Quaternion run

Perpetual Circle multiform and mix

And nourish all Things; let your ceaseless Change

Vary to our great Maker still new praise.

Ye Mists and Exhalations! that now rise

From Hill or standing Lake, dusky or gray,

Till the Sun paint your fleecy Skirts with gold,

In Honour to the World's great Author rise;

Whether to deck with Clouds th' uncolour'd Sky,

Or wet the thirsty Earth with falling show'rs,

Rising or falling still advance his Praise.

His Praise, ye Winds! that from our Quarters blow,

Breathe soft or loud; and wave your Tops, ye Pines!

With ev'ry Plant, in sign of Worship, wave.

Fountains! and ye that warble as you flow

Melodious Murmurs, warbling tune his Praise.

Join Voices all ye living Souls, ye Birds!

That singing, up to Heav'ns high Gate ascend,

Bear on your Wings, and in your Notes his Praise

Ye that in Waters glide! and ye that walk

The Earth! and stately tread, or lovely creep;

Witness if I be silent, Ev'n or Morn,

To Hill or Valley, Fountain, or fresh Shade,

Made Vocal by my Song, and taught his Praise."

Thus I have given a short account of all the sorts of poems that are most used in our language. The acrostics, anagrams, &c., deserve not to be mentioned, and we may say of them what an ancient poet said long ago,

"*Stultum est difficiles habere nugas,*

Et stultus labor est ineptarum."

FINIS.

Milton Keynes UK
Ingram Content Group UK Ltd.
UKHW012315040624
443649UK00020B/570